FOUNDATIONS FOR FUTURE SUCCESS

Book 1

Table of Content

INTRODUCTION

Enter the realm of "Foundations for Future Success," an exploration of the core of self-improvement and self-control. This is not your normal self-help book; it's a dynamic toolbox I created using knowledge from professionals and my own experiences. With every page you turn, you're moving closer to being a more successful, confident, and fulfilled version of yourself.

Start by reading "Unlocking Connection" to learn more about effective communication. Here, we dissect the art of meaningful conversations, covering everything from our voices' powerful resonance to our nonverbal signs. It's not only about talking; it's also about being heard and realizing how important communication is to your life. Learn how to make decisions and solve problems in "Problem Solving and Critical Thinking." As you gain the ability to handle problems with grace and originality, turn setbacks into chances for personal development and creativity.

Dive into the intricacies of empathy and teamwork with "Developing Effective Relationships." Learn the techniques for fostering fulfilling and fruitful relationships, focusing on the transforming potential of emotional intelligence in interpersonal and professional interactions.

Finally, master time management techniques and organizational skills by reading "Managing Time and Responsibilities." Learn how to manage the many obligations of contemporary life, including how to deal with stress and how important it is to put your health first. Every page is designed with thought-provoking stories, useful tips, and interactive exercises, all delivered in a conversational style that humanizes and makes even the most abstract concepts approachable. This book is a partner on your path to success, not just a book.

Your journey through "Foundations for Future Success" is a call to accept change, face obstacles head-on, and realize your greatest potential. Your book is here to support you every step of the way as you set out on your transforming journey; remember, it's your route to success, so have an open mind and heart.

"The only limit to our realization of tomorrow will be our doubts of today." – Franklin D. Roosevelt

CHAPTER ONE

Unlocking Connection: The Power of Effective Communication

Greetings and welcome to the study of effective communication, a fundamental path that is essential to your pursuit of personal development. In this chapter, we take on the role of your guides as we navigate the complex dynamics of words and gestures that influence our day-to-day encounters. Think of every discussion as a creative brushstroke on the canvas of life, where the words you use have the power to enlighten and connect.

We begin by discussing the power of questions, like shining spotlights, and how they can help us make sense of our ideas and encourage more in-depth introspection in our information-rich society. A well-phrased question can start a person on a path of significant self-discovery and reveal previously undiscovered information.

Imagine your opening remarks in any conversation as the first notes of a large symphony. Every exchange can be transformative, emphasizing not only rhetorical skill but also the tactical use of reasoning as a navigational tool, especially in the turbulent waters of highly charged arguments.

Emotions, the lifeblood of our conversation, take center stage. Transforming your words into authentic feelings transforms a straightforward message into a meaningful and impactful exchange of ideas. If you have a young, energetic vibe, then let your enthusiasm come through in your words and invite others to join you in your colorful world. Together, this spirit of adventure promotes the investigation of fresh concepts and viewpoints

Metaphors and analogies function as intermediaries between ideas, converting abstract ideas into approachable stories. Recognize that this is a mutually beneficial journey that involves building relationships beyond the pages of this book.

With common sense as our guide, we negotiate the challenges of reducing complicated concepts to understandable ideas and creating a common ground between opposing viewpoints.

As we work through these chapters, your task is to turn learned knowledge into practical actions. Can you use the knowledge you've received to direct your future?

Pop culture allusions serve as allies in our journey, anchoring our understanding in the spirit of the times. Simplicity fosters clarity in communication, bringing even the most complex conversations to light.

Use the energy of the young to turn every interaction into a chance for inspiration and personal development. Recognize the critical role that communication has in advancing the world; use your words to shed light on and motivate change.

Every inquiry we ask and every reflection we do on our journey of self-discovery through good communication becomes a purposeful step toward our personal development. When it comes to learning the skill of connection and transformation, this guide is your ally. Now let's get the conversation started!

The Art of Effective Communication

Amid the ever-changing fabric of our modern society, clear and concise communication becomes crucial in helping us navigate the maze of miscommunications and confusion. It is more than just art; a plethora of studies from the fields of psychology, sociology, and anthropology support its scientific status.

Let's look at some specific data: according to Albert Mehrabian's research, 93% of communication occurs non-verbally and only 7% occurs verbally. Body language (55%) and tone of voice (38%) make up this non-verbal component, which highlights the fact that the way you communicate frequently has a greater impact than the content of the message.

Imagine a dispute as a tactical battleground where your words are soldiers and your tone and body language are the tactics of attack. A skilled communicator knows that a confident tone can be more compelling than the most poetic speech, that leaning forward indicates participation, and that keeping eye contact indicates honesty.

But communication is a debate, not a one-way street. Studies in sales, a profession that depends largely on communication, demonstrate the importance of active listening, with top salespeople dedicating over 60% of a conversation to listening. Why? Whether you're selling a product or building connections, the key to effective interactions is knowing what other people need and meeting those needs.

You can improve your communication abilities by using this methodical approach:

- Engage Your Ears in Active Listening: Gain insight into the feelings and intentions or meanings that lie beneath the words.
- Empathize: Put yourself in the other person's position to understand what they are thinking or why they are thinking the way they are.
- Body Language Awareness: Your posture, gestures, and facial expressions convey a lot about you. Pay attention to them. Also pay attention to other speakers.
- Speech Clarity: Keep your words succinct and to the point; waffling loses impact.
- Feedback Loop: Seek and offer helpful criticism from others; it's a two-way learning process.

Be prepared for the odd error—misunderstandings are a necessary element of learning. Like learning to ride a bike, every bad conversation is a step toward being a better communicator because it teaches you about balance

Anthropological research confirms that communication has always been at the center of human society, from the complex clicking languages of the ancient San people to the fast-paced activity of Wall Street. The thread that connects people on a human level is effective communication.

As you go, keep in mind the power of words, the nuances of nonverbal cues, and the skill of active listening. These resources will help you succeed in many areas of your life, from building strong relationships to acing job interviews. Communication is more than just sharing information; it's about bridging the gap between our experiences as humans and uniting us in ways that go beyond words.

Setting off on the complex path of successful communication, we are about to reflect and explore the nuances that form the craft of connection. Imagine profoundly connecting moments, talks that go beyond words, where ideas come together like tributaries to form a powerful river of understanding. In those cases, you are addressing the fundamentals of successful communication.

Still, turn back the hands of time and remember times lost in cacophonous noise—a meaningless language duel. These situations exemplify the paradox of communication: it is a talent that may either strengthen a relationship or cause it to fall apart.

Why is this mysterious event happening? What magic turns one exchange of words into a melodic sonata and another into a raucous crescendo? Fundamentally, communication is a complex art, a symphony that is not only composed of words but also of inflections, silences, and nonverbal cues.

Think about the digital world, where modern hieroglyphs are electronic signals. Have you ever considered the implications of sending a straightforward SMS before clicking the send button? Every individual is a stroke on the canvas of your connections, expressing meaning, intention, and emotion. Your muse is waiting to be unleashed; the potential of great communication is only a reflective pause away.

Think of each interaction as a brushstroke you make on the canvas of relationships, like an artist carefully selecting brushstrokes and colors to evoke certain feelings. With every word choice, textual color, and expressive detail, you too may create a masterpiece, just like a painter uses their tools with skill. The world of effective communication is full of possibilities, like a blank canvas waiting for your skillful touch.

Let's examine the digital environment as we move forward—a place where acronyms, GIFs, and emoticons coexist peacefully with words to create a vibrant tapestry of expression. What effect do these symbols have on the message's depth? Consider how your relationships have been impacted by this world of screens; it molds your online persona altering in person relationships and interactions.

Like a mosaic, the structure of communication is complex and each piece adds to the overall picture. We'll examine both verbal and nonverbal indicators, as well as spoken and unspoken cues, in the upcoming chapters as we break down this mosaic. We'll work together to unravel the strands that make up a meaningful conversation, empowering you to become a great communicator.

Before we go any further, take a moment to reflect: In what way do you approach a conversation? What dictates how you interact? What hues would you like to apply to your communication canvas? These inquiries will serve as our compass during this intriguing communication adventure.

Think about the nature of communication: it is a complex ballet of expressions, gestures, and sentiments rather than merely a verbal interaction. These components come together to create the elusive nectar of insight in a magnificent symphony. The unwritten language, or nonverbal hints, gives every discourse dimension. We explore critical thinking here, which is your guide through this maze-like environment.

Put yourself in a situation where everyone is sharing their points of view in a group discussion. Pay attention to body language, word emphasis, and tonal changes while you listen. By using critical thinking, you can decipher their complex meanings. Given enough observation, time, and practice you can also learn how to use your own communication skills to inject changes in conversations that can impact everyone, altering the trajectory of the message and the efforts of the participants.

Take a moment to reflect: How frequently do you delve deeper into conversations? How sensitive are you to the nonverbal signs that go along with spoken language? Your ability to accept this complexity deepens your understanding of how people interact.

Like a jigsaw puzzle, communication is made up of snugly fitting words, gestures, and pauses. Also, like any great puzzle, the more complicated the picture, the more pieces you must use and the more intricate it becomes as it is pieced together for everyone to see. Step into the world of storytelling, where you become a storyteller in the truest sense. Your words create a mental picture for your audience.

Now set out on a journey of reflection: How frequently do you notice clues that are not spoken during conversations? How does this observation affect the way you understand things? How does being able to read between the lines strengthen your relationships? What does "read between the lines" mean to you?

It takes both keen observation and active participation to unlock the code of meaningful relationships. Pay attention to pregnant pauses, tone inflections, and changes in mood in addition to spoken words. When you go beneath the surface and explore the many layers below, magic happens.

Imagine a metaphorical dance, where nonverbal clues are elegant pirouettes and words are choreographed steps. You can intentionally infuse every word you say.

Stop, and examine your verbal attempts. To what extent do you study nonverbal cues? You explore depth and comprehension when you encourage critical thinking. The mosaic of connections is made up of a symphony of cues rather than just spoken words.

Consider a calm pond with an intricate biosphere underneath it as a metaphor for productive dialogue. Quite simple on the surface, but rich in depth for those who are prepared to delve into it.

Think back to a time when you were moved by someone's remarks. Their message resonated because of the harmony between simplicity and profundity. The ability to express complex ideas clearly and concisely is the foundation of effective communication.

Think about having a real conversation, sharing more than just your opinions. Being self-aware is essential. Think about the feelings or emotions of the listeners before speaking out loud. To what extent does your message correspond with your intention and their emotions or feelings? Will your message persuade, dissuade, or change things entirely?

Imagine a situation where you choose emotional honesty over going into specifics. "I feel frustration because my connection to this matter runs deep." A doorway into your soul, tremendous depth can be found in simplicity.

Communication simplicity is an art of distillation rather than a submission to shallowness. Like a chef choosing components for a masterpiece, every phrase adds taste and togetherness to the expression, resulting in a harmonic whole.

Start a contemplative investigation: How often do you listen to your feelings before speaking? In what ways does verbalizing emotions help or hinder interactions? Even seemingly straightforward words have deep meaning.

Consider the impact of a well-selected quotation—a phrase that captures entire spheres of ideas. Your words can spread understanding. How can you incorporate your experiences into stories that others can relate to?

How skillfully do you combine depth and simplicity in your expressions? Bring in sincerity and openness. Complex or verbose communication isn't always the correct choice, sometimes simple conversations is a powerful tool that can have tremendous impact; the choice of which to use and when requires careful consideration.

Think back on the recent discussions. Have you ever felt the need to elaborate when a few simple words would have done? Incorporate simplicity without sacrificing complexity. You adopt a communication style in this skill that strikes a chord, establishes a connection, and creates a lasting impression. Being simple is not a facade; rather, it is the starting point for a profound journey of self-awareness and human connection.

Unlocking Nonverbal Communication: What Actions Say

Imagine a world where comprehension transcends speech, where communication dances not only on lips but also in the silent spaces between. A world where words control everything. Imagine breaking the good news to a buddy and watching as their expression paints a picture of happiness with big smiles, large eyes, and a joyful stance. Here, spoken language and the unseen art of nonverbal communication coexist harmoniously.

Consider how your daily encounters are shaped by your body language. A small change in stance can convey hesitation or confidence. During a conversation, leaning in conveys volumes, much like the final notes of a symphony resonate.

Now enter a scene where you say something to a family member that seems a little bit frustrating. Your tone conveys depth and intricacy, much like a melody does for words. Take a moment to consider how effectively you can read your tone of voice and your body language. Examine the communication canvas you create with each nonverbal brushstroke. Consider what your words say versus what your body says, are they delivering the same message?

Think about the impact of a well-placed pause in a conversation—a silent interval that invites thought or an answer. It serves as a blank canvas on which others can draw their ideas and combine them to create a masterpiece of dialogue.

While you go about your day, take note of the nonverbal fabric surrounding you. A smile changes people's perception of words. How does your posture affect what you're saying, my dear reader?

Think beyond words to the intangible, the feelings that precede language. Said another way, communication is a tapestry of visible and invisible strands, not only spoken words.

Go ahead and consider GIFs and emojis in the digital age. How can an emoji change the tone of a text message? Make deeper written exchanges by utilizing these symbols.

Uncovering a deeper understanding of the people in your life through nonverbal communication is a singular experience. Examine yourself. How frequently can you interpret nonverbal cues? How can you improve your relationships with this silent language? Examine the silent vocabulary, my friend, and strengthen your relationships.

As you fully engage in this conversation, keep in mind that communication is not limited to spoken words. Investigating nonverbal clues is similar to piecing together a fine tapestry—it reveals the connections that lie just beneath the surface.

To convey feelings, ideas, and intentions, nonverbal cues are essential. The following twenty-five cues should be noted:

1. Expressions on the Face: Eye rolls, frowns, raised eyebrows, and smiles all convey feelings and reactions.

2. Eye contact conveys curiosity, confidence, or discomfort depending on its intensity and duration.

3. Body Posture: Your standing and sitting positions convey your level of assurance, focus, and apprehension.

4. Gestures: Pointing and hand gestures highlight spoken words.

5. Handshakes: Firmness and strength communicate respect and confidence.

6. Personal Space: Keeping oneself apart from others denotes security, familiarity, or limits.

7. Touch: Hugs and back pats convey varying degrees of closeness and affection.

8. Nodding: Shows attentive listening and participation.

9. Head Tilt: Expresses curiosity, empathy, or interest.

10. Mirroring: Mirroring body language conveys a sense of connection and rapport.

11. Changes in Posture: Abrupt adjustments convey uneasiness, defensiveness, or discomfort.

12. Crossing one's arms: Shows discomfort, resistance, or defensiveness.

13. Leaning Forward or Back: Leaning forward indicates involvement, whereas leaning back indicates ease or disengagement.

14. Touching Face: Indicates trepidation, doubt, or introspection.

15. Finger tapping: Indicates restlessness or agitation.

16. Clenching one's fists: Manifests anxiety, annoyance, or a need to regulate feelings.

17. Shake your head: Expresses disapproval, incredulity, or rejection.

18. Shifting Weight: Expresses unease or irritability.

19. Smirking: A little smile conveys humor or distrust.

20. Leg Cross: Indicates defensiveness or relaxation.

21. Foot Movement: Irritation or restlessness is indicated by tapping or wriggling.

22. Raise Your Shoulders: Show fear, trepidation, or uneasiness.

23. Touching Hair: Playing with one's hair might convey flirting or uneasiness.

24. Maintaining Proper Posture: An upright stance exudes assurance and self-belief.

25. Looking Around: Continual glances around indicate discomfort or distraction.

Gaining an understanding of these nonverbal clues is similar to having the ability to decipher other people's feelings and intentions. It's an ability that promotes deeper understanding and improves communication.

You can navigate the unspoken language that dances beneath the surface of spoken words by being aware of these tiny cues. Imagine being able to tell whether a buddy is uncomfortable by seeing a small change in posture or by observing the real interest reflected in someone's eyes during a conversation. These cues contribute levels of subtlety to every interaction by creating a silent dialogue that sometimes supports spoken language and other times contradicts it.

Gaining an understanding of non-verbal signs makes you a more sympathetic communicator. You comprehend not just what is being said, but also the feelings that are underneath it. You can establish a deeper connection because it's like getting a behind-the-scenes look at the feelings that go into the performance.

Furthermore, there are two sides to this consciousness. You can interpret the nonverbal cues as well as modify your nonverbal cues to more accurately describe your goals and feelings. Your non-verbal cues become an effective tool for communicating yourself, whether it's a solid handshake to convey confidence or keeping eye contact to demonstrate real interest.

Knowing these cues is like learning the rhythm in the complex dance of human contact, where words and gestures waltz together. It makes it possible for you to follow or lead with grace, maintaining harmony in dialogue. There are fewer misunderstandings and more opportunities to establish genuine connections with people.

Thus, keep in mind that active engagement—rather than passive observation—is essential when you set out to decipher non-verbal language. If you observe how words and gestures flow together, you'll discover that you're building deeper connections that weave knowledge and communication together.

Navigating the Sea of Relationships: Building Better Relationships

Consider yourself the captain of a massive vessel, preparing to embark on a historic voyage across the immense ocean of interpersonal connections. Imagine yourself navigating a complicated universe of interactions, and imagine that good communication is your reliable compass, guiding you through the highs and lows of relationships.

Recall a moment when you were chatting with a new acquaintance when it developed into a meaningful discussion of ideas. That is the wonder of effective communication: it is a dynamic journey that reveals common ground and fosters comprehension.

A crucial component of this journey is empathy. You can enter into another person's emotions and see things from their perspective when you listen with true empathy. Reading the emotions like stars in the sky to guide you is like navigating a sea of relationships.

Consider conversing with a family member who holds a different belief system now. You accept the power of attentive, engaged listening rather than engaging in a heated debate. You create bridges across differences by using open-ended inquiries as a compass to understand one another.

Take a moment to reflect on your conversations. How frequently do you try to comprehend rather than persuade? How may empathy alter your interactions with other people? As you continue reading, allow empathy to play a major role in forming your relationships.

Let's now discuss active listening, which is a wonderful technique that involves paying close attention to what the other person is saying and experiencing throughout a conversation while tuning out outside distractions. Your lighthouse will be active listening as it steers conversations toward genuine participation.

Keep this in mind as you navigate the relationships sea: effective communication involves listening and understanding as much as speaking. It involves figuring out the subtle currents that bind your experiences to those of others. By actively listening, you give the speaker the priceless gift of your whole attention and convey that you value what they have to say.

Consider the impact of probing queries. When you inquire, "What values matter to you here?" or "How are you feeling?" You delve further, examining the profound feelings and viewpoints. It's similar to finding buried gems amid a sea of discourse. Let's now take a closer look at relationships and productive communication. Consider it as spelunking unknown caves in the sea of connections.

Your compass in this enormous ocean of emotions is empathy, which will lead you through the ups and downs. Consider conversing with a friend who is experiencing a difficult day. You can assist them in navigating rough seas by listening to them with empathy, just like a co-captain might. Amid a sea of difficulties, your comprehension serves as an anchor for them. Reflect on the times when you just needed to vent, and a friend continued offering advice when you only needed them to silently listen. Reading emotions and non-verbal clues can help you to become the anchor you wanted.

Think about how important it is to have an open mind as you proceed on your trip. Approach conversations with an open mind, just like a sailor eager to explore new waters. Your voyage will be richer and more colorful if you embrace the range of viewpoints and ideas as the vivid marine life beneath the sea's surface.

Let's now venture into the domain of impactful inquiries. Consider using inquiries like "What inspires you?" or "What challenges have you overcome?" to delve deeper than simply asking basic questions. These inquiries take you to the undiscovered riches of people's viewpoints and experiences, much like treasure maps.

Imagine talking with a friend about your dreams. Your words take on the shape of sails that capture the wind of support and encouragement. The ocean of talk becomes a place where hopes meet and dreams sail together, forming a common path toward goals.

Think of gifs and emoticons as your crew members in the age of digital technology. They give your communication style and joy, transforming your exchange into a vibrant dance on the waves of technology. Emojis function as your contemporary signals, expressing emotions in a lively and imaginative manner, much like sailors would with flags when commingling at sea.

Effective communication is an ongoing journey rather than a destination, so keep that in mind as you navigate the dynamic sea of relationships. Every discussion is an opportunity to learn more, become closer, and reveal the secrets that add character to any relationship.

So, embrace the skill of communication as your compass on this thrilling journey of relationships, set your sails high, and remain open to the wonders of the sea. Cheers to your journey, Connection Explorer!

Empowerment Through Connection: Unleashing the Power of Your Voice

Imagine yourself at a fork in the road, where you find the superpower of empowerment combined with the broad field of personal growth. Your voice becomes a guiding light here, illuminating the path ahead. It's like being in a mystical place. Communication becomes your bright guiding light on this road of change, enabling you to speak up, close knowledge gaps, and forge meaningful connections.

Recall an instance where your words had an impact and your voice was powerful. It starts meaningful conversations and causes change to ripple like stones dropped into a serene pond. This is the core of communication-based empowerment—a potent instrument that enables you to utilize your voice to advance both personally and globally.

Now picture yourself as an expert navigator navigating over challenging terrain. Communication turns into your super toolset as you travel through your conversations. It assists you in accurately and stylishly expressing your requirements, desires, and goals. Making a genuine difference and being heard and understood are more important than merely speaking.

Imagine yourself in a heated debate with a diverse bunch of people, each with their own opinion. You find common ground through good communication, which unites these disparate points of view. Amid difference, your words act as skillfully constructed bridges that foster understanding and harmony.

Take a moment to reflect on your own life. How frequently do you take the risk to voice your opinions, share your dreams, and defend your needs? How can effective communication increase the volume and impact of your voice? Let's consider the various ways that communication empowers us to control and lead our narratives as we examine this chapter.

Let us now discuss the participatory aspect of empowerment. Envision a workshop where individuals discuss and exchange ideas and experiences. You participate actively in the conversation by offering your insights, rather than merely observing. It's through these interactions that people grow personally and a feeling of community emerges.

As you progress through personal development, consider the subtle yet effective impact that reflection plays. Imagine yourself sitting beside a calm beach and observing the waves. These reflective times are not merely idle idleness; they are windows through which you can make sense of events, identify areas for personal development, and acknowledge your accomplishments.

Now consider the power of well-crafted inquiries. When you ask yourself questions like "What do I want to accomplish in my life by age 50?" "What steps can I take to reach my goals?" or "How can I make a difference?" By introducing critical thinking, you're laying the groundwork for independent action. Your journey to becoming the finest version of yourself is illuminated by questions like these.

Gaining empowerment via communication is a collaborative process that involves speaking, listening, and expressing yourself. Think back for a moment on your most recent experiences. How frequently do you empower yourself and the people around you by using your communication skills? How can you use your voice as an instrument for good in the world?

Never forget that communication is your ship on the voyage of self-discovery that is personal development. It's the ship that will help you sail through the choppy seas of connection and empowerment. Most importantly, the ship you weather the storms of life with should always be yours and not borrowed from someone else.

Remember that communication is more than simply a tool as you continue on your path of self-discovery and personal development; it's the ship that takes you across the wide ocean of growth. See this ship as a solid craft that is sailing the choppy seas of empowerment and connection.

Your ability to communicate effectively serves as a sail on the turbulent waves of life, capturing the breezes of comprehension and guiding you toward deep connections. It's the ship that gives you the confidence to share your dreams, express yourself honestly, and overcome obstacles on this exciting journey.

Let's treasure and honor the moments of reflection—those occasions when you sit on the edge of your mind and look out at the ocean of life. These experiences serve as anchors that keep you in the here and now so that you can reflect on your path, identify your strengths, and chart your own direction for the future.

Consider stimulating conversations as your ship's vibrant crew. Every conversation and idea exchange join this vibrant community and helps make your journey a success. They combine to provide the bright energy that helps you move forward. However, you should never forget, you are the captain of your own journey and every decision you make should always be your own.

Consider this introspection and interactions as the charts and compass directing your vessel. Thought-provoking discussions serve as compasses, guiding you toward development and connection, while reflections serve as maps, assisting you in navigating the geography of your inner world.

Consider how your voice can influence the enormous ocean of human experience as you sail toward empowerment through meaningful relationships. Your ship becomes a guide for those navigating their waters as well as a tool for personal development. Through your genuine communication, you inspire others to start their self-discovery journeys.

Let's embrace the reflecting and engaging aspects of this amazing experience as we go on. They serve as the maps and compasses that lead us to the desired goal of empowerment via meaningful connections.

Balancing Realism and Resonance: Navigating the Art of Communication

Knowing what to say, how to say it, and when to say it is the art of communication. You're still learning this skill as a teenager. Realistic but impactful communication is what you want to convey.

Being realistic entails speaking the truth and being open and honest. Don't say things merely for impact, embellish tales, or exaggerate. Speak honestly and plainly. Credibility and trust are increased in this way.

However, resonance is also very important. Your speech should have a profound effect on the audience. Truth and facts alone are insufficient; your message is enhanced by empathy, feeling, and personal significance.

Find the ideal balance between resonance and realism. Give individuals relatable details from actual life. When communicating, consider whether what you're saying will benefit the other person or just feed your ego. How will they feel about it? Make your message relevant to their experience.

You'll become proficient at speaking empathetically and realistically with practice. When it's acceptable, be honest. Learn to interpret nonverbal cues from tones and body language. When folks are open to it, schedule important conversations. Add a little humor to lighten the situation.

Two-way communication is necessary. Pay close attention, be patient, and show compassion. Think things over before you answer. This striking mix of resonance and realism will make you stand out as a perceptive and considerate communicator.

One of the primary means of daily communication that we use is conversation. Excellent conversational skills are important whether interacting with friends or meeting new individuals. Finding the right balance between reality and resonance is essential to becoming a conversational expert.

When you converse, try to be genuine. Engage and be present with the person you are speaking with. Pay close attention to what they have to say instead of simply waiting for your moment to speak. Make meaningful follow-up inquiries that demonstrate your interest. When appropriate, share your personal experiences and tales; however, avoid embellishing or oversimplifying the information. Credibility and trust will increase if you continue to be honest and open.

Making emotional connections is also important if you want your interactions to have resonance. Thus, let loose a bit! Share your thoughts, feelings, and dreams with others so they can relate. Be open to deeper conversations and willing to be vulnerable rather than merely engaging in trivial talk. When conversing with friends or in a business setting, use a more informal and relaxed tone and vocabulary.

Acquire the skill of interpreting nonverbal cues from people by focusing on tone and body language in addition to spoken words.

Do they have their attention focused or diverted? Feeling grateful or uninterested? By answering correctly, you can resonate more effectively. Use comedy to lighten the situation if they appear closed off. Hold off on discussing delicate subjects until it is appropriate.

Recall that there is reciprocity in discussion. Ask questions and pay attention instead of just talking about yourself. Give advice only when specifically requested. Give them space to be silent comfortably rather than interrupting them. Finding a balance between being genuine and establishing deep relationships is key to being a successful conversationalist.

A sophisticated communication talent is navigating challenging talks. It takes tact and consideration to handle disagreements, critiques, and harsh realities. But when done well, you can have meaningful talks about even the most sensitive subjects.

Set the scene first by waiting for the right moment and location—likely to occur while passing or in public. Keep your composure and kindness. Begin by reaffirming your good intentions and common interests. Remain impartial and non-judgmental when listening. Avoid interjecting.

Before you react, ascertain all the details. Keep opinions apart from the real world. Be tactful but honest. When you disagree, concentrate on arguments rather than criticism. If feelings are strong, step away. Hurt feelings can be acknowledged without getting worse.

When possible, establish common ground and go from there. Nobody wins all the time, and making a compromise is not weak. Express sincere regret for any offense caused. Reaffirm your intention to continue the relationship afterward.

Following up shows you care - check on how they've been feeling since. Did they reflect more on what was discussed? Do they need support? Reassure that you can handle disagreements maturely.

Difficult conversations take courage but are invaluable for growth. Be realistic yet resonant by debating issues with empathy. Staying calm, keeping an open mind, and finding compromise leads to mutual understanding - strengthening your bond.

How you present yourself communicates a lot about who you are. First impressions matter, so make them count! Balance an authentic presence with resonance when introducing yourself to stand out.

Lead with realistic confidence - self-assured but not cocky or arrogant. Share a firm handshake, eye contact, and warm smile. Speak clearly and avoid self-deprecating humor initially. Listen attentively when others talk.

Open up gradually to resonate emotionally. As conversation flows, look for chances to show passion for interests, goals, or causes. Share inspiring experiences from your life. Be thoughtful in what you reveal about your personality and values.

Adapt your presentation based on the situation. In professional settings, dress neatly and avoid profanity or controversial topics. Loosen up around friends with inside jokes and stories. Modulate volume and body language accordingly.

Handling conflict gracefully also leaves a good impression. Don't get riled up by differences of opinion. Hear them out, then respond calmly with reason, logic, or facts. Do not take opinions personally or perceive them as factual, every person has their own unique view of the world. Be a mature, rational presence in tense moments.

Ultimately, presenting your best self is about consistency - being real yet putting your best foot forward. Maintain self-respect, stand up for your principles, and lead by example. These qualities will resonate and speak volumes.

Finding your unique voice takes self-discovery. As you gain life experience, stay true to yourself while crafting how you want to be perceived.

Start by assessing your values, passions, and goals. What issues get you fired up? What change do you want to see in the world? Why? How? Use this foundation to shape your voice and stand for something.

Define the tone you want to convey. Leader-like? Quirky? Thought-provoking? Whatever fits your personality. Just keep it genuine - forcing something contrived is obvious.

Refine your voice through practice. Write, speak, and create content that resonates with your message. Fine-tune language, style, and delivery for maximum impact. Listen to feedback to improve without compromising your core self.

Use your voice responsibly. Promote empathy, not exclusion. Challenge ideas, not people. Amplify other voices along with your own. Wield your voice as a force for good; one that seeks to unite rather than divide.

Staying true to your voice builds courage and clarity. It acts like a magnet, drawing others who vibe with your authentic self-expression. Your voice is power - use it wisely.

Your Challenge Ahead: Elevating Your Communication Prowess

The foundation of successful cooperation, leadership, and professional growth are the abilities that define good communication. One of the most potent transferable talents is excellent communication. However, we frequently discover that we struggle in different areas when it comes to communicating.

Have you ever struggled to articulate your thoughts clearly, leaving your audience perplexed? Or perhaps you've experienced the frustration of not being heard, your valuable insights falling on deaf ears.

These are just a few examples of the pain many of us face in our communication journeys. However, the good news is that these challenges are not insurmountable. With the right tricks and techniques at our disposal, we can transform our communication skills.

The art of communication is a dynamic one. Remember that if you approach discussions with the correct mindset, even the most boring ones can turn into stimulating exchanges as you travel along. Every exchange offers the opportunity to develop, learn, and make deep connections. Let's take a moment to think through your strategy before you go off on this path of reflection and improved dialogue. How often do you start a discussion with a sincere interest and a voracious appetite for detail? Just take time to examine how you communicate: the words you use, how well you listen, and the relationships you try to build. Where is it that you shine and where do you think you could be better?

Imagine yourself in a communication garden, where each exchange blossoms into a singular, magnificent flower just waiting to be discovered. Your curiosity-driven approach can bring these discussions to life by revealing the profound layers that lie beyond the surface, much like a curious botanist discovering the hidden glories of a floral world. How could you bring this curious spark into your conversations to start thought-provoking conversations and create deep connections? Develop a curious mindset first. Show that you are genuinely interested in this. Pose meaningful queries that demonstrate your desire to learn more. Observe other people's stories rather than drawing attention to yourself. Examine their beliefs, anxieties, and dreams. This encourages introspection.

Try to talk half as much as you listen. Waiting for your turn to speak is not enough. Take in viewpoints that differ from your own. Give up making assumptions, since assumptions are considered to be the mother of all __ ups. Take a moment to completely digest before answering. Permit moments of pleasant stillness. Listening provides you with an understanding that speaking cannot.

Seek common ground while validating the experiences of others. Everybody has a basic urge to feel important and like we belong. Acknowledge common goals and challenges. Encouragement should be given. This quickly establishes rapport.

Conviction in your convictions is important at the same time. When it comes to matters of conscience, be kind but strong. When handled appropriately, differences of opinion don't pose a threat. You can expand your horizons even in contentious debates

Pick your words well, but don't worry too much about being perfect. Talk honestly and from the heart. It can prove your sincerity when you stumble over words. Examine the subtleties inside the text. Subtleties, body language, and tone of voice can convey deeper messages. Are they attentive, preoccupied, or grateful? Make the appropriate adjustments to your strategy. The secret is emotional intelligence.

Arguments may certainly come up. Be composed and set a good example. Avoid meeting animosity with more animosity. Recognize the hurt sentiments, but shift the focus of the conversation back to problems rather than personal assaults. If feelings become too strong, take a break.

Choose your battles carefully. Not every disagreement calls for a heated discussion. Think about the conflicts with real consequences. To what extent does debating issues of pure choice help?

When appropriate, use comedy to lighten the situation. Laughter relieves stress. Lightheartedness and perspective can be restored with a well-chosen joke or story. But be careful not to derail delicate conversations.

Recall a time when a question brought you to a complete stop and prompted in-depth introspection. Can you still feel that pause, that instant when everything appeared to stop around you and you were left to think on your own? What new perspectives have this introspective trip given you on the world and your role in it? These stimulating queries are similar to keys that open doors to introspection. They put your viewpoints to the test and inspire you to delve deeply into your ideas and convictions. You may have discovered fresh information and peeled back layers of self- and world-awareness in that reflective zone.

Imagine now using this self-reflection technique in your regular conversations. Envision using it seamlessly in your talks to take them to a whole new level. What if, when you interact with people, you ask thought-provoking questions that set off a conversation about self-reflection?

Think about how deliberate questioning affects the depth of your discussions. These inquiries serve as links, establishing a deep connection between you and other people. They create a bond that goes beyond the surface by encouraging a shared investigation of concepts, emotions, and viewpoints.

Using the practice of self-reflection in your relationships has a transforming effect. It's about co-creating a space where real conversations take place, not merely exchanging ideas. Through this exercise, the conversation reaches new heights where empathy expands, understanding develops, and connections get richer. Give these thought-provoking questions some serious thought; the answers will open up a wealth of richer communication. Ask these provocative questions of friends and family and pay close attention to what they have to say. Take note of the nuances, such as the kaleidoscope of expressions, the carefully chosen phrases, the thoughtful pauses, the tone of their voice, and non-verbal signs.

You are not merely hearing words when you see their responses; rather, you are translating feelings and experiences into a language that makes sense. Words alone might not fully convey the depths of emotions and ideas that are shown by the subtleties in their answers. It's similar to reading a gripping narrative in which the silences have equal weight with the words.

After this enlightening exchange, move the discussion along. Talk to them about how you understand their answers, and establish an atmosphere of open communication. Talk about your observations and hear what they have to say. A greater comprehension of their viewpoints, feelings, and life experiences is fostered by this approach.

Together, you will travel a path of mutual understanding and connection as you examine the nuances. It's a cooperative investigation of the human experience rather than merely a conversation. You develop closer relationships with others and acquire a deeper understanding of the nuances of their emotions and ideas through this conversation.

So, feel free to utilize these queries as starters for in-depth discussions. Discover what's hidden beneath the surface, and allow the sharing of interpretations to build a bridge that strengthens your relationships. These times of mutual reflection weave a thread of empathy and understanding in the tapestry of enriched communication.

1. What do you think is the most important quality a person can possess, and why?
2. Can you describe a time when you faced a difficult decision? How did you go about making that choice?
3. Imagine you're stranded on a deserted island with only three items. What would those items be, and how would you use them to survive?
4. If you could have a conversation with any historical figure, who would it be and what would you ask them?
5. Reflect on a time when you felt truly understood by someone. What did they do or say that made you feel that way?
6. If you had the power to change one thing about the world, what would it be and how would you go about making that change?
7. What's a moment in your life that significantly shaped your perspective or values?
8. Imagine you're allowed to meet your future self. What questions would you ask them?
9. If you were to write a letter to your younger self, what advice or insights would you offer?
10. What's a misconception or stereotype that you've encountered in your life? How did it make you feel?

11. Think about a person you admire. What qualities or traits do you admire most about them?

Be aware of the small details when interacting with friends and family, such as non-verbal clues, tone, word choice, pauses, and expressions. These are designed to be thought-provoking questions. By talking about how you understand their answers, you'll learn more about their thoughts, emotions, and experiences. A stronger bond and more fruitful communication may result from this adventure.

Gaining communication skills requires commitment but pays off greatly. Continue investigating, hearing, and thinking. Take in revelations like a flower takes in sunlight, letting every exchange feed your never-ending thought garden. Envision a society in which thoughts go unspoken, partnerships break down because of miscommunication, and poor communication stunts professional advancement. None of us could survive in that world. Unquestionably, effective communication is essential to our success in the workplace.

CHAPTER TWO
Problem Solving and Critical Thinking

Greetings, sharp minds! You've entered a fascinating chapter that is brimming with intellectual energy. This chapter extends an invitation for you to explore the world of critical thinking and problem-solving, where the attraction of adventure unfolds and your intelligence emerges as the brave intellectual knight in dazzling armor.

Let's go out on this exciting adventure with a fascinating curiosity. Have you ever been enthralled with the dancing of the constellations in the night sky and wondered how they manage to navigate the vastness of the universe? Think about this: every heavenly riddle, every starry sentinel, offers a convergence of enigmatic obstacles. However, the astronomers are the ones who deftly solve these cosmic riddles. What if I told you that you are similar to these cosmic navigators in your intellectual journey?

Imagine yourself as a cosmic navigator, exploring the unknown lands of knowledge and comprehension as you plunge into the wide ocean of intellectual study. You have the same tools to solve the complex riddles that are in front of you as do those who can interpret the language of the stars.

Think about the difficulties faced by celestial navigators: the great distances, the intricate patterns, and the constantly shifting cosmic landscape. In the same way, you come across challenging issues and complex puzzles in the field of critical thinking that beg you to investigate and solve. You use your brain as a compass to navigate these uncharted territories.

Now, let's apply this analogy to the majesty of adventure. Picture your intellectual path as an adventure filled with quests and quests within quests. Each challenge you encounter becomes a stepping stone, propelling you forward on this epic odyssey of the mind.

In the same way as heavenly navigators advance our comprehension of the universe, your quest for analytical thinking and problem-solving advances humankind's collective knowledge. You turn into a truth-seeker, an insight-finder, and a participant in the epic story of human intellect.

Embrace the adventure that comes with investigating, delving into, and solving the secrets that surround you in this chapter of cerebral vitality. Your mind is a dynamic force that shapes the features of your intellectual landscape; it is not just a passive observer.

Thus, bright minds, allow the sparks of inquiry to fan the flame of your curiosity. Explore the vast expanses of knowledge, solve the puzzles of the stars, and become the scholar-priest whose pursuit of knowledge enriches the fabric of human thought. There's an adventure ahead of you, and your brain will be your guide across these unexplored territories of knowledge. Brave brains, let us advance to the splendor of intellectual exploration!

Mastering Problem Solving

Greetings, fellow seekers of knowledge and self-improvement, as we begin a chapter titled "Mastering Challenges: The Art of Problem Solving," which is filled with insightful advice on overcoming life's complex obstacles. This section serves as your doorway to deciphering the secrets of conquering setbacks using the invaluable resources of fortitude, flexibility, and steadfast resolve.

Remember a time when an impassable barrier seemed to overwhelm you? Think about the tactics you used, the stances you took, and the victory that ensued—a demonstration of the depths of your inner fortitude. This chapter's pages expand as we examine the art of problem-solving, revealing techniques that enable you to not just survive but also thrive in the face of life's complex puzzles—much like an adventurous traveler navigating unfamiliar territory.

Before we embark on this thrilling adventure, let's ask ourselves a basic question: What is the essence of problem-solving, and why is it so vital to our existence? Think of it as a talent, a superpower that gives you the capacity to break down complex problems into smaller, more manageable parts and create workable answers. It is the secret of converting hardship into opportunity, difficulties into learning opportunities, and uncertainty into lucid understanding.

Imagine that when we peel back the layers of problem-solving, you are painting solutions with the brushes of imagination and logic on a canvas. It's not only about solving problems; it's also about accepting the journey and developing an attitude that sees obstacles as opportunities to demonstrate your creativity and fortitude rather than as barriers to overcome.

Think of solving problems as a dynamic, uncertain tango or dance in which every step is a calculated step toward a solution. It pushes you to uncover the underutilized parts of your talents and abilities and to embrace the discomfort of the unknown.

Now picture problem-solving as a link between information and action, a means by which your understanding and insights become meaningful changes. It moves you beyond mere academic understanding, urging you to use your intelligence in real-world circumstances, transforming problems into chances for growth and progress.

Learning how to solve problems well is like knitting tenacity, adaptability, and determination into the very fabric of your life if you will. It's a transformative skill that prepares you for today's challenges and paves the way for a day when your aptitude for navigating complexity will be recognized as a sign of intellectual and personal mastery. So, my fellow travelers, let's journey to the core of the art of problem-solving—a journey that offers enlightenment, growth, and the unparalleled fulfillment that comes from conquering life's difficult obstacles.

Have you ever wondered about the complex relationship that exists between addressing problems and the vastness of the human experience? Imagine that every option you make is a chance to use your problem-solving skills. Problem-solving is a constant companion on life's journey, whether you're tackling global concerns, pursuing your aspirations, or navigating the complexities of relationships.

Imagine for a moment that you are an artist, and that your decisions and solutions are the brushes you use to paint the masterpiece that is your life, rather than a blank canvas. Every brushstroke adds nuance and vibrancy to the story of your life, creating a picture of your experiences that reflects your never-ending development. The problem to solve is what will your masterpiece look like when you finish.

Think about how important flexibility is when it comes to fixing problems. Consider it the skill of adapting to changing circumstances without breaking. Knowing when to change course, when to press on, and when to take an innovative approach is an essential component of problem-solving, much like a sturdy tree in a storm.

How does empathy fit into this complex picture? Empathy acts as a link between your solutions and other people's hearts and thoughts. It serves as a prism through which you can understand their viewpoints, wants, and emotions. When you have empathy, your solutions become more than just practical—they become compassionate.

See your life as an epic adventure, with each obstacle representing a dragon that needs to be defeated. Solving problems becomes your weapon of choice—your sword, shield, and armor—a means of overcoming social, intellectual, and personal challenges. By improving your problem-solving abilities, you too can succeed, just like a knight does while facing a strong opponent.

Imagine now a future in which people use their ability to solve problems to address global concerns. Polution, inequality, and poverty are enormous problems that require large-scale group problem-solving. By becoming skilled at this craft, you become more than just a hero in your narrative; you become an advocate for a better society and a part of the group that works to create a more promising and sustainable future. Dear reader, as you delve into the depths of this chapter, remember that problem-solving is not just a skill but a philosophy, a way of life. It's your passport to personal growth and a compass guiding you through life's labyrinthine challenges. So, let's embark on this journey together, ready to conquer obstacles, create solutions, and craft a life filled with purpose and achievement.

Take a pause and let your thoughts drift back to those moments when life presented you with a puzzle, a dilemma, a riddle that seemed to defy your understanding. It could have been that perplexing math problem, a thorny personal conundrum, or a tricky social situation that felt like navigating a labyrinth. In this chapter, we're diving headfirst into the exhilarating world of problem-solving, where the art of overcoming obstacles is a thrilling adventure of curiosity, creativity, and resilience.

Picture this: You're handed a puzzle, its pieces scattered like stars in the night sky, seemingly unrelated, chaotic. But instead of turning away, your curiosity ignites a spark. You want to unravel the mystery, decipher the hidden patterns, and bring order to the chaos. This curious, enigmatic dance is at the very heart of problem-solving—the relentless quest to seek understanding, grasp the elusive solutions, and construct meaning from seemingly disparate parts.

But let's rewind for a moment. Can you recall those times when a problem felt like an impassable mountain, a maze with no exit? These are the moments where critical thinking steps onto the stage. Critical thinking is your trusty guide through the intricate labyrinth of challenges. It's the beacon of reason that illuminates the darkest corners, helping you dissect complex problems into manageable fragments and offering a multitude of perspectives.

Now, you might wonder: Why is this skill so essential? What does it mean to truly master the art of problem-solving? The answer lies in the realm of personal development. Each problem you encounter, each obstacle you surmount, is a stepping stone on the path of your growth. Through problem-solving, you become more adaptable, more resilient, and better equipped to navigate the unpredictable waters of life.

Imagine the process of constructing a puzzle—a thousand tiny pieces, each one a fragment of a greater picture. Much like assembling a puzzle, problem-solving is a process of exploration and experimentation. It's about venturing into the unknown, testing hypotheses, and embracing the thrill of discovery. Your willingness to embark on this explorative journey is your gateway to innovative solutions.

Here's a thought to ponder: What if every challenge is an opportunity, a hidden treasure chest of growth and self-improvement? Much like a sculptor who chips away at a rough block of stone to reveal a magnificent statue, you too can carve your challenges into stepping stones toward personal development. The power to solve problems lies within you, waiting for you to embrace it.

As we continue our exploration, let's consider the multifaceted nature of problem-solving. How do you approach challenges? What strategies do you employ to break them down into digestible morsels of understanding? How do you harness your unique strengths and talents to discover solutions? Take a moment to reflect on your experiences and how they resonate with the lives of fellow teens who are navigating the labyrinth of problem-solving just like you.

The intricacies of problem-solving are akin to a labyrinth—a maze of twists and turns, each corner presenting a new riddle. Throughout this chapter, we'll chart the labyrinth's pathways: the strategies, the mindsets, and the tools that will empower you to navigate complexity with confidence and creativity. Together, we'll untangle the threads that weave the tapestry of mastering challenges, guiding you toward a horizon of self-discovery and resilience.

So, before we plunge deeper into the realm of problem-solving, take a moment for introspection: How do you react when faced with a challenge? What strategies have you employed in the past? What skills and mindsets do you aspire to cultivate as a formidable problem-solver? Keep these questions close as we embark on this curiosity-fueled journey, for they will be your compass in the captivating world of problem-solving.

Take a moment to immerse yourself in a profound truth: life presents us with a dazzling array of challenges, each unique in its complexity and significance. Embarking on the path of problem-solving mastery requires embracing this diversity of challenges while nurturing the deep well of resilience within you. Whether the challenge is as mundane as a puzzle or as intricate as a complex life decision, each one serves as a canvas upon which you can paint the vibrant strokes of your personal growth and development.

Let's traverse the corridors of memory and revisit a time when you grappled with a problem demanding more than just ordinary solutions. Perhaps it was a school project that begged for innovative approaches, or a personal quandary requiring an extra dash of ingenuity. In those moments, problem-solving reveals its enchanting nature, beckoning you to strike a harmonious balance between the realism of the challenge and the tantalizing possibilities of creative resolutions.

Now, cast your imagination into a scenario where you confront a riddle, a puzzle so intricately woven that it defies the conventions of conventional logic. As you begin to peel back its enigmatic layers, your imagination takes flight, venturing into uncharted territories of possibility. This imaginative exploration breathes life into problem-solving – it's the exhilarating quest to expand the horizons of what's deemed plausible, to dare to entertain solutions that exist beyond the realm of the ordinary.

Pause for a moment and direct your gaze inward. How frequently do you embark on the adventure of problem-solving, gracefully straddling the realms of realism and imagination? When faced with challenges that beckon for creative thinking, how does your response manifest? These questions demand your contemplation, for your ability to navigate this finely balanced complexity is the key to elegantly traversing the intricate maze of problem-solving.

Imagine problem-solving as the art of constructing a bridge. Just as a seasoned engineer must meticulously consider a multitude of factors – physics, materials, and design – in crafting a sturdy bridge, so must you carefully weigh a myriad of variables when confronting the challenges of life. The bridge you forge acts as the vital link connecting the chasm between the problem that confronts you and the elusive solution you seek

Now, cast your thoughts toward the realm of innovation. When a scientist embarks on the journey of discovery, they blend their existing knowledge with an insatiable curiosity and a dash of imagination. In the realm of problem-solving, you too are an innovator, and your mind serves as the laboratory where you conduct experiments, dissect complexities, and synthesize ingenious solutions.

Here's a question that will stir your contemplative faculties: How do you master the delicate art of balancing realism and resilience while navigating the labyrinth of problem-solving? When a challenge materializes on your horizon, how does your mindset transform, and what role does your creativity assume in shaping your approach? Ponder deeply the interplay between the practical and the possible, for therein lies the key to unlocking ingenious solutions.

Empowering Solutions: Embracing Mastery in Problem Solving

Consider this investigation of the essence of personal development as an empowerment journey, where the art of problem-solving serves as a beacon of guidance that illuminates your route. It gives you the tools to take on life's obstacles head-on, coming up with winning plans and paving the way for achievement. Remember that your journey toward personal development is both empowering and reflective, a mirror reflecting your inner growth, as we delve deeper into the insightful investigation of this chapter.

Just take a moment to consider building a bridge. Everything has a purpose, from the strong base to the elegantly curved beams that span the space. In a similar vein, problem-solving involves building a mental bridge—a bridge that links the current problem and the desired solution. Your attitude and tactics turn into the key elements, guaranteeing that your bridge is strong and durable enough to weather the storms of misfortune.

Now, allow your mind to wander as we imagine the following scenario: Imagine yourself in front of a complex problem with no obvious way out due to its intricate design. Your only guide through its maze-like passageways will be your critical thinking. This indispensable tool acts as your guide, guiding you through the maze-like maze of turns and twists and skillfully assisting you in navigating the challenge's complexity.

Critical thinking serves as a compass in this maze of personal growth, guiding you while also motivating you to figure out the puzzle's hidden connections and patterns. It forces you to think critically, assess, and come up with new ideas, breaking down the seemingly insurmountable into a sequence of doable tasks. As you make your way through this maze, you come to understand that problem-solving, which is based on critical thinking, is a skill that turns obstacles into chances for development and education.

Imagine now that personal growth is like a sculptor creating a masterpiece, and every obstacle is a chisel that helps you become a better version of yourself. The outlines of your trip are shaped by the skill of problem-solving, which is closely linked to critical thinking. Let every answer you come up with as you go through the twists and turns paint a picture of your personal development, telling a story of resiliency, flexibility, and victory.

As we continue our in-depth investigation, remember that problem-solving is more than just a method; it's a way of thinking that sees obstacles as opportunities to grow and transform into a more capable and mature version of yourself. It is the dynamic force that drives you forward, transforming the personal development journey into an empowering experience and a mirror of your inner transformation.

Take a minute to think back on the difficulties you've overcome in the past. Go back to the rush of success, the gratifying feeling of development that rushed through you as you figured out a solution. It's important to understand that this feeling of empowerment is a result of your remarkable capacity to become proficient at problem-solving, which will enable you to not only survive but also thrive in the face of life's challenges.

Now imagine this comparison: addressing problems is likened to tending a colorful garden. You are the gardener in this mental garden, tending to a range of tactics and abilities, giving them tender loving care. With time, your toolkit for addressing problems grows and blossoms, bearing a bountiful harvest of answers to the problems that crop up in your life.

Examine your methods for solving problems for a moment. How do you empower yourself in the face of life's challenges? How do you overcome adversity by utilizing your special talents and abilities? You can take a step toward being a proficient problem solver who can confidently and easily navigate life's curveballs by adopting the many solutions we'll explore in this chapter.

Think about the complexity of issues that affect not just your own life but also the lives of your friends, peers, and perhaps your family as we continue our research. How do these challenges speak to you personally, and how could they impact others differently? Think about how you create solutions that align with your goals and dreams. Consider how your journey through problem-solving reflects on the experiences of your peers as a whole, creating a web of development and knowledge exchange.

Keep in mind that fixing problems is a collaborative process. You take on issues head-on, put your well-practiced tactics to use, and watch as problems turn into solutions. Imagine yourself sitting behind a keyboard, expertly arranging notes to create a symphony. In a similar vein, you are a composer of answers, arranging your abilities and perceptions into tasteful conclusions. Every note that is played in this interactive symphony of problem-solving adds to the melody of personal growth, resulting in a melodic composition that reflects the resiliency, flexibility, and success that are intrinsic to your path.

Empowerment is a process of constant growth and resilience, going beyond the simple purchase of solutions. Imagine that every obstacle you overcome becomes a rich soil in which the seeds of your empowerment sprout and grow. By learning to traverse the complex maze of problem-solving, you develop the skills necessary to face life's uncertainties with poise and confidence.

Think of empowerment as a flower opening up, with each petal standing for a lesson acquired, a skill refined, and a challenge conquered. The ability to solve problems creatively serves as this flower's sunlight, enabling it to reach its full potential. As you overcome each obstacle, you not only find answers but also discover your inner strength, which builds a strong sense of competence and self-assurance.

Accept the deep potential of problem-solving as more than just a tool and allow it to serve as your compass on the endless journey toward self-improvement. See it as a compass that points you in the direction of personal development and self-discovery while guiding you through the oceans of doubt. Your ability to solve problems effectively becomes your sails, capturing the winds of change and taking you to new places.

Consider every obstacle you face along this journey of transformation as a chance to become more powerful. Every issue you resolve shapes the story of your tenacity, flexibility, and success. Your path of personal development is like a symphony, with the notes of problem-solving harmony creating a tune that reflects your journey's tenacity, adaptation, and triumph.

Thus, let the immense ability to solve problems serve as your compass, lighthouse, and guiding light as you journey toward personal growth. As you take on challenges, you not only find answers but also discover hidden strengths that build a strong sense of competence and self-assurance. Let the skill of problem-solving guide you through the uncharted territory of personal development, shining a bright light on your journey through empowerment.

Reflecting on Solutions

It is crucial to understand that addressing problems effectively is a much deeper process than just coming up with answers; it involves reflection and personal development. This journey through difficulties serves as a mirror, revealing aspects of your personality, the effectiveness of your plans, and your capacity for change. Remember that reflection is the compass that will help you navigate the complex maze of problem-solving as we explore this chapter.

Consider the comparison to navigating a big ocean. An experienced sailor uses both cunning and flexibility in addition to navigational aids to successfully negotiate the erratic seas. Similar to this, addressing problems requires you to navigate a sea of difficulties while being alert, changing course when necessary, and drawing significant lessons from your mistakes.

Imagine the following situation now: You're faced with a problem that doesn't appear to have an obvious answer and find yourself at a crossroads. Your reliable ally as you analyze this complex problem from several perspectives is critical thinking. It grounds you in a realm of strategic thinking and logical reasoning, serving as your anchor.

Take a minute to turn back time in your life's narrative and concentrate on a recent obstacle you faced. What strategy did you use? Which tactics did you skillfully apply? Look at the result now. What important lessons did this event teach you? Problem-solving becomes much more than just a task during this introspective process of thought; it's a meaningful chance for learning and development.

You use reflection as a lens to examine the decisions you made, the routes you followed, and the results you obtained. It asks you to consider the development of your intellectual and emotional faculties as well as the efficacy of your tactics. During this introspective process, problem-solving turns into a dynamic force that helps you overcome obstacles and molds your own story, which adds to the continuous tale of personal growth.

Let reflection be our continuous companion as we make our way through the complex maze of problem-solving; it will serve as a guiding light that reveals the lessons hidden inside each obstacle. The symphony of progress and self-discovery produced by the combination of problem-solving and reflection reverberates through the personal development chambers. Accept this life-changing experience, where every obstacle turns into a chance for self-reflection, every resolution serves as a springboard, and every contemplation serves as a guide to the infinite possibilities of lifelong learning and personal growth. Consider addressing problems as the fascinating process of piecing together a jigsaw puzzle that contains hidden pieces. Every task gives you pieces of these hidden clues and challenges you to figure out the answers. By attempting to put these puzzle pieces together, you not only overcome obstacles but also piece together a more comprehensive knowledge of your mental processes and cognitive capacities.

Now for a thought-provoking question: How frequently do you look introspectively at your experiences addressing problems? To what extent are you able to distill nuggets of insight from these problems, regardless of how quickly or slowly they were resolved? Think about how reflection plays a major role in your development as an expert problem solver.

Changing our focus to the field of science, scientists use introspection to draw relevant conclusions from data and experiments. In a similar vein, you are also a student of the craft of problem-solving. You can derive great wisdom and insights from your experiences by using them as raw materials.

Think about the complex concepts that surface as you make your way through the reflective waters. How does fixing problems relate to your quest for personal growth? How do you take the lessons you learn from obstacles and use them in your next interactions? Consider how your realizations align with the complex dance of conquering obstacles.

Solving problems is a life-changing journey that challenges you to go to new places, think critically about what you already know, and adjust to the ever-shifting swells of hardship. You travel into the unexplored regions of your mind, uncovering fresh viewpoints and methods for solving life's mysteries, much like an adventurous traveler exploring unfamiliar territory.

We're going to go on an exciting journey together in the upcoming chapters, where you'll learn a ton of tactics, ways of thinking, and methods that will help you become an expert problem solver.

Never forget that fixing problems is a journey that involves more than just finding answers—it's a voyage of resilience and personal development. Every obstacle presents a chance to not only find answers but also to explore new aspects of yourself, making the journey of problem-solving a rewarding and life-changing experience.

Consider the process of addressing problems as a dynamic tapestry containing strands of intelligence, flexibility, and resilience. Every obstacle you face is a different pattern in this complicated design, calling you to decipher its intricacies. The process of solving problems is an ongoing investigation into who you are. The interaction between difficulties and solutions serves as a blank canvas on which you can draw the bright lines of personal development.

Think of the process of addressing problems as a conversation between your future, present, and previous selves. The obstacles you have overcome are like ghosts of the past, echoing with lessons learned that inform your choices and deeds of the present. At the same time, every solution you create serves as a guide for your next interactions and provides an understanding of how your problem-solving skills are developing.

Let's make analogies to the literary world in the same spirit. Each issue you face is a new chapter full of surprises and character growth in the book of your life. The narrative thread that gives the plot consistency is your attitude to problem-solving; it transforms obstacles into turning points that influence the overall narrative of your personal growth.

When you set out on your life-changing adventure, picture problem-solving as a symphony in which every obstacle presents a different tune. Your answers are like notes on a piano; they blend to form the background melody of your development. Consider the tempo and cadence of your problem-solving symphony—how every obstacle brings a fresh dimension, and every resolution enhances the dynamic work of art that is your life.

Problem-solving appears as a recurrent theme—a motif that echoes across the chapters of your life story—in the broad tapestry of your personal development. It's not just about getting over problems; it's also about developing a mindset that adapts to new situations and grows stronger every time. Your problem-solving path is a story of continual self-discovery, perseverance, and empowerment.

Allow your mind's ink to flow freely as we go more into the study of problem-solving methods and approaches. Think of the difficulties that lie ahead as chances to add new lines to the epic poem of your growth rather than as obstacles to be conquered. Accept every challenge as an opportunity to learn and apply critical thinking and creative problem-solving skills, and let the experiences of life unfold into a symphony of solutions, wisdom, and progress.

Your Challenge Ahead

Let's take a moment to contemplate before you go out on this cerebral voyage. Think about the way you now negotiate the choppy waters of life's problems. Do you feel like a seasoned captain navigating your ship, or are you lost and alone in unfamiliar waters? Identify the tactics that come to you naturally and those that still need to be found and refined.

As you explore the upcoming material, keep in mind that solving problems is a dynamic ability that shapes your growth rather than just a work to be completed. Think of it like a toolkit with different instruments, each intended to handle a different kind of problem. Not only do your efforts depend on how well you use these tools, but also on how much development and resilience you develop in the process.

Think of this investigation as a treasure hunt, where every chapter offers fresh perspectives and methods to improve your toolkit for solving problems. While some tools might seem familiar to you, others might be lurking around the corner, just waiting to wow you with their power. Accept the variety of these methods because the secret to solving problems successfully is found in combining them.

Imagine yourself as an architect creating the blueprint for your problem-solving attitude as you turn the pages ahead of you. Consider the pillars that underpin your present strategy and be willing to strengthen or modify them. You have the chance to hone your problem-solving abilities and build a sturdy foundation for personal growth, much as a master artisan refines his instruments to perfection.

This is an interactive interaction with the story of your problem-solving journey, not just a passive reading experience. Make it a challenge to use the tactics and knowledge you've learned in practical settings. Think of each situation as a workshop where you hone your craftsmanship in problem-solving and enable your abilities to progress from theory to real-world proficiency.

The difficulties you face are not obstacles to prevent you from moving forward, but rather stepping stones that will help you achieve more self-awareness and mastery. Accept the journey, acknowledge your accomplishments, and draw lessons from your failures. You have the chance to create your growth symphony through the complex dance of problem-solving, transforming obstacles into melodious solutions.

So, as you prepare to set sail into the seas of problem-solving exploration, let the compass of reflection guide you. Understand where you stand, envision where you aspire to be, and embark on this odyssey with the eagerness of a pioneer, for the challenges ahead are not obstacles but gateways to your transformative evolution.

Critical Thinking

Ladies and gentlemen, prepare yourselves for an engrossing journey into the world of self-discovery and personal development as you board this cerebral waterway. Here, the skill of critical thinking serves as the expedition's lantern, illuminating the way for a life-changing voyage motivated by curiosity and a desire to learn.

Imagine your mind as a vast, uncharted territory that is full of mysteries. Your critical thinking will serve as an invaluable tool to help you navigate the complex mental terrain. You can use critical thinking to map the uncharted regions of your ideas and thoughts, much as explorers use their equipment to navigate uncharted territory.

One may wonder why critical thinking is so important. Consider it as your personal development's fuel, the cognitive engine that propels your ability to assess, analyze, and decide wisely. In the same way, that a perfectly tuned engine can launch a rocket into space, critical thinking may help you reach new heights in personal development.

Let's now consider the forks in your life that you have had to cross. Have you ever been unsure of your course of action? In these situations, critical thinking steps forward as your unwavering compass, clearing the numerous paths in front of you and helping you make deliberate, well-informed decisions.

Consider this analogy: critical thinking enables you to create your thoughts and ideas into sophisticated and meaningful forms, much like a sculptor meticulously transforms a block of stone into a masterpiece. It turns unpolished ideas into brilliant nuggets of understanding, serving as the chisel and hammer in your mental workshop. Consider every stone an idea that has been carried in by someone, but only you as the master artisan, through critical thinking can analyze each stone and determine if it is has real value or if the person offering it to you, is claiming it has value because they want it to.

However, how can critical thinking show up in our day-to-day activities? Think of it as the secret ingredient that turns an easy recipe into a fine dining experience. It improves your ability to analyze difficult problems, pinpoint underlying causes, and come up with workable solutions. It also allows you to be selective about what ingredients or information is useful or valuable and what ingredients can slowly poison a dish and everyone who consumes it.

Allow every wave of information and curiosity to carry us forward as we forge ahead through the unexplored waters of critical thinking. The trip that lies ahead will not only be one of intellectual study but also one of transformation, with the ability to think critically acting as a wind in our sails to help us reach new heights in self-awareness and personal development.

Let's now engage in a reflective question: to what extent do you engage in critical thinking on a conscious level? Is it something you notice when you make decisions? Think back to the times when you were guided by critical thinking to move from a state of bewilderment to a clear understanding. Think about how many times an adult, media source, or educator may have presented something as fact, but it didn't quite sit well with you. Maybe you had a feeling that the information wasn't accurate or wasn't entirely accurate.

Consider critical thinking as a set of binoculars that provide you with an exceptionally clear and sharp view of far-off places. It enlarges your viewpoints, much like this optical equipment, so you can find hidden details and make better decisions. By looking closer at the presented information, you can find where it might not be cohesive. Maybe it is sewn together to create a different image when you don't look closely.

As we explore the vast field of critical thinking, consider the various themes that are there. In what ways do you apply critical thinking to problems about your personal growth? How does it influence the way you connect with the outside world? Consider how this mental compass can guide you on your life's journey through its many curves.

We will go further into the practice of critical thinking in the upcoming chapters, revealing methods, approaches, and attitudes that will enable you to use this potent instrument with effectiveness. But remember, reader, that this is a journey of self-discovery and personal development, not just a quest for knowledge. Critical thinking is the North Star that points the way to a more enlightened and promising future.

Your Call to Action

Please pause for thought before we begin this in-depth investigation of critical thinking. To what extent are you aware of your capacity for critical thought? Can you think of any situations in which it was crucial to your choices and actions? Let these reflections be your mental compass as you make your way through the upcoming chapters, directing you on this life-changing path of self-improvement. Welcome, dear reader, to the fascinating journey of critical thinking, a voyage into the depths of your intellectual prowess. Picture this as an exhilarating quest, where the sword of curiosity is your weapon, and the armor of discernment protects you from the pitfalls of misinformation and superficiality.

But before we delve deeper, let's pause for a moment and ponder: When was the last time you found yourself entangled in a web of questions, trying to solve a complex problem or unravel a perplexing issue? Critical thinking is your beacon of light in these moments, the trustworthy guide that illuminates the path through the labyrinth of your thoughts and the complexities of existence.

Now, picture this scenario: you're presented with a puzzle, a mosaic of ideas, facts, and perspectives that appear scattered and disjointed. Yet, your curiosity acts as the spark, urging you to piece together this intricate mosaic. This quest for connecting the dots, for unveiling hidden patterns, lies at the heart of critical thinking – the relentless pursuit of intellectual clarity and understanding.

But let's rewind to a different scene: a moment when you came across a situation that seemed awry, a claim that didn't quite add up, or a piece of information that raised your eyebrows. It could have been a dubious advertisement, a dubious statement, or a news story that left you with more questions than answers. In such instances, critical thinking emerges as your armor, protecting you from the snares of misinformation, manipulation, and deceit.

Now, you might be wondering: why is critical thinking a vital skill in your arsenal? What does it mean to be a critical thinker, and how does it tie into your journey of personal growth and development? The answer lies in the profound impact it has on your life. Critical thinking is your key to unraveling complexity, enhancing problem-solving skills, and becoming a wise and discerning decision-maker.

Consider how often society might tell you something to sway your decisions in a way that benefits its agenda. Marketing companies say whatever they can get away with, if it means you will buy their products. Politicians say whatever they think the people want to hear, if they think it can get them elected. Critical thinking allows you to hear what is being said but not accept it blindly as indisputable facts. Critical thinking only survives when users wield it to challenge narratives and reveal the truth which is often obfuscated.

Think of it as your investigation into the mysteries of life. Just as a detective pieces together fragments of evidence to solve a case, critical thinking empowers you to gather facts, analyze data, and arrive at sound conclusions. It is your inner Sherlock Holmes, leading you toward enlightenment.

Now, let's dive into a philosophical question: What if every challenge, every enigma you encounter, is an opportunity to exercise your critical thinking skills? Much like a detective piecing together the puzzle of a crime, you can use critical thinking to decode the mysteries that life presents. The power to think critically lies within your grasp, awaiting your embrace.

As we embark on this exhilarating journey, consider the multifaceted themes of critical thinking. How do you approach the torrent of information that inundates your daily life? How do you sift through the deluge of data, distinguishing fact from fiction and discerning truth from fallacy? Reflect on how your experiences resonate with the experiences of fellow adolescents, for critical thinking is a universal tool for navigating the complex tapestry of existence.

As you embark on this journey through the intricate landscape of your mind, envision it as a sprawling terrain, with hills of insight and valleys of uncertainty. At its core, critical thinking is the compass guiding you through this intellectual expanse, helping you chart a course toward clarity and enlightenment.

Consider this: the human mind is a vast repository of thoughts, beliefs, and ideas. It's like a vast, uncharted wilderness. Within this mental wilderness, critical thinking acts as your intrepid guide, leading you through the dense forests of doubt, across the wide plains of ideas, and up the cliffs of understanding. It empowers you to uncover the layers of thought that lie hidden beneath the surface, just waiting to be explored.

Think back to those moments when you engaged in spirited debates or discussions. Whether the topic was a pressing social issue, a thought-provoking book, or a complex scientific concept, critical thinking was your steadfast companion. It nudged you to question assumptions, explore alternative perspectives, and articulate your ideas with clarity and conviction.

Now, picture this scenario: you're faced with a multifaceted problem, a conundrum with multiple solutions, each carrying its unique set of consequences. In such moments, your critical thinking skills emerge as your guiding star, illuminating the path toward well-informed decisions. It helps you weigh the options, anticipate outcomes, and choose the most suitable course of action.

Pause for a moment and reflect on your daily life. How frequently do you consciously engage in critical thinking beyond the walls of academia? How do you approach the challenges that pepper your everyday existence with a discerning mind? It's in your willingness to embrace this complexity that you enrich your ability to navigate the intricate terrain of thought.

Imagine critical thinking as an elaborate toolbox for the mind. Just as a skilled craftsman employs a range of tools to shape and refine their work, critical thinking equips you with the mental tools necessary to refine your thoughts, solve problems, and make well-grounded decisions.

Consider the art of interpretation. When a musician interprets a piece of music, they breathe life into the notes, infusing emotions into their performance. Similarly, you, too, are an interpreter when you engage in critical thinking. You decipher the intricacies of information, dissect arguments, and unveil the hidden meanings within.

Now, let's plunge into the depths of introspection with a profound inquiry: How frequently do you consciously exercise your critical thinking skills? How does it alter your comprehension of the world that surrounds you? How does the mantle of critical thinking empower you to navigate the labyrinth of information and ideas?

To unravel the secrets of critical thinking, you must become a keen observer of your thoughts and the world itself. It involves not just questioning information, but asking the right questions. The real magic of critical thinking lies in this domain—where you move beyond the surface to explore the intricate layers beneath.

Imagine critical thinking as a puzzle, where each piece of information is a puzzle piece, and your mind serves as the board.

Just as you assemble these pieces to form a coherent picture, critical thinking enables you to arrange scattered information into a clear and meaningful understanding.

Take a moment to evaluate your critical thinking habits. How frequently do you question assumptions, evaluate information, and delve into situations that demand discernment? How often do you hear or read something and then repeat it to others, blindly without validating if the information is true or accurate? By embracing critical thinking as a daily companion, you are embarking on a profound journey—a journey that transcends mere acceptance of information at face value and delves into the symphony of cues that compose the complexity of human thought.

In our dynamic and complex world, a timeless saying captures a crucial skill: "Trust nothing that you hear and only half of what you see." This advice was more than just a saying; it was a critical survival tool in historical times when discerning truth from falsehood was vital. In the present day, the importance of this philosophy is undiminished, particularly for someone young and curious like you.

Accepting information without scrutiny means relinquishing a fundamental power: the power to form your own beliefs and shape your destiny. Imagine a scenario where every piece of information is taken at face value without question. In such a world, true innovation and progress would stall, and the diversity of thought and ideas would diminish.

As a young person developing your critical thinking skills, you have the ability to alter this scenario. You can cultivate a mindset that thrives on asking in-depth questions, diligently verifying sources, and weighing different perspectives. Such a critical approach not only prevents you from being swayed by popular but unexamined opinions but also develops you into a well-informed individual. Your ability to think critically and analyze information critically becomes a valuable asset to society.

Your journey through skepticism and rigorous inquiry is not merely about challenging what others say; it's about challenging your own understanding and views. This process of continuous reflection and questioning doesn't just make you a follower of pre-existing paths; it turns you into a trailblazer, guided by a deep knowledge and a zest for inquiry. Embrace this path of critical thinking, and observe how it not only enhances your understanding of the world but also positions you as an active participant in shaping its future.

Imaginative Exploration: Beyond the Boundaries of Thought

Embark on an enthralling odyssey through the realms of critical thinking and imaginative exploration—a journey that transcends the confines of conventional thought and spans the vast expanse of possibility. Envision this grand adventure as a tapestry woven with the threads of curiosity and creativity, where your mind becomes the compass and map guiding you through uncharted territories of limitless potential.

Critical thinking, in its essence, is not a static endeavor shackled to the analysis of existing information. It's a dynamic process that beckons you to push the boundaries of your thoughts, encouraging you to envision what lies beyond the horizon. It serves as the spark that ignites innovation, the key to unlocking novel solutions, and an indispensable facet of personal growth.

Close your eyes for a moment and picture a world where everyone complacently accepts the status quo without ever questioning or imagining a different reality. It's a stagnant world, bereft of progress and innovation. Now, let your imagination take flight as you contemplate the boundless possibilities that emerge when critical thinking joins forces with imaginative exploration. Consider how this union empowers you to question, to wonder, and to dare to dream of a brighter, more transformative world.

Engage in introspection and ponder: How frequently do you tread the path of imaginative exploration? How do you nurture and foster your innate creativity and curiosity? Recognize that your willingness to embrace this delicate balance between critical thinking and imagination enriches your capacity to navigate the intricate labyrinth of human thought.

The creative investigation is similar to the bold expedition of exploring unknown territory. Like adventurers venturing into the unknown to uncover uncharted territory and uncharted possibilities, you set out on a mental journey into the depths of your thoughts. This is where you find new ideas and creative fixes that are just waiting to be discovered.

Think about the nature of innovation. When someone invents a novel tool, they imagine a time when their creation will completely transform people's lives. In the same way, creative discovery is the path to innovation. Your thoughts are the change seeds; your ability to think critically is the fertile ground in which those seeds grow and bear fruit.

Imagine the harmony of creative exploration and critical thinking as a dance as we move through this chapter. While imaginative inquiry adds the hues and vibrancy that turn the ordinary into the extraordinary, critical thinking gives the structure and logical foundation.

Think of the world of art as a canvas that is brought to life by imaginative brushstrokes that adhere to design principles. Similarly, your mind becomes a blank canvas ready to be painted with the brush of inventive investigation, with critical thinking serving as the compass that gives the shape and substance of your artistic creation.

Now apply this metaphor to your day-to-day activities. Consider every choice and every obstacle as a blank canvas ready to be painted with your deliberate, imaginative masterpiece. Take part in the delicate dance between creative discovery and critical thinking, and watch as your life transforms into a colorful tapestry of growth and creativity.

We shall delve into the details of this complex interaction between critical thinking and creative discovery in the upcoming chapters. We'll look at methods, approaches, and perspectives that will enable you to maximize the combined strength of these two powerful forces. Always keep in mind, dear reader, that this is not just a conceptual exploration; rather, it is a life-changing journey of self-discovery and enlightenment, with the combination of critical thinking and creative exploration serving as your compass.

Together, we will delve deeply into the complex dance between critical thinking and creative exploration, revealing the threads that entwine creativity and personal development into your intellectual landscape. As we go into this investigation, we urge you to contemplate and reflect on the enormous influence of letting your imagination thrive in tandem with your critical thinking.

For a brief while, picture your mind as a large landscape that is just ready to be painted with rational and creative strokes. The ever-dependable brush of critical thinking carefully draws the contours of your ideas, offering organization and clarity. However, creative inquiry, like bright paint, gives these ideas vitality, color, and depth, turning them into a masterwork of original ideas.

Imagine yourself as the painter and the canvas to fully understand this connection. Your mental environment is built on the logical framework of critical thinking. It examines, breaks down, and assesses to make sure the foundation is solid and the framework is sound. But when creative research is combined with imagination, that's when the real magic happens. It presents the nuances of potential, the nuances of uncharted territory, and the luminosity of innovation.

Now let's get to the main question: How frequently do you let your creativity run wild alongside your analytical thinking? This dynamic interaction is a means of developing into a visionary thinker rather than just a simple mental workout. It challenges you to push past preconceived notions and bravely venture into the wide ocean of the unknown, where creativity and novel viewpoints are waiting to be discovered.

Think about the comparison between a sculptor molding a marble block. As the chisel, critical thought precisely and purposefully carves out the intricacies. However, the sculpture comes to life thanks to creative exploration, which turns an inanimate block into a piece of art. In a similar vein, your mind becomes a playground for original concepts and imaginative solutions when it is fostered by both critical thinking and imaginative exploration.

Consider how you now engage in creative exploration. How frequently do you allow your mind to stray, to wonder, and to dream outside of your comfort zone? Your ability to solve problems creatively and imaginatively is locked away in this delicate balance between critical thinking and imagination.

Engaging in imaginative inquiry can improve your problem-solving skills by presenting a multitude of viewpoints and answers that might not be immediately evident when viewed solely through an analytical lens. It pushes you to think beyond the box, consider different possibilities, and welcome the unusual. Your mind becomes a kaleidoscope of possibilities throughout this dynamic process when new concepts emerge and previously undiscovered areas of thought open up.

As you walk the path of personal growth, realize that critical thinking is more than simply an analytical tool—it's the lighthouse that points you toward the endless opportunities that lie ahead. Accept this dichotomy as a strength that will help you think creatively and logically as you go toward original solutions and comprehensive problem-solving.

Interactive Challenge: Balancing Thought and Imagination

It's more than simply a workout when you take on The Interactive Challenge: Balancing Thought and Imagination; it's an exploration of your innermost intelligence. Imagine this interactive inquiry as a dynamic process that smoothly combines creative exploration with critical thinking as you get started.

Start by deciding on a subject that interests you. It can be a work of art that stirs strong feelings in you, a technological development that piques your interest, or a social issue that makes you curious. The key is to pick a topic that challenges your thinking and forces you to learn more.

Take a minute to pick up your pen or open your digital notepad, keeping your chosen topic in mind. Letting your critical thinking take center stage is the first step. Start by drafting insightful questions regarding the selected topic. To fully understand the topic and all of its nuances, these inquiries ought to go beyond the obvious and penetrate deep into the subject. Consider questions that could alter the perceptions, intentions, or consequences of your topic. Dive deep into questions that need to be asked but others haven't thought to ask or tried to answer yet.

You are letting your critical thinking abilities direct the preliminary stages of the investigation as your queries take shape on the page. This is like putting the points on your mental map and identifying the area you are going to go through. Your attention is guided toward the important facets of the subject by the questions, which act as a compass.

Now that you have established a list of inquiries, it is time to go into the domain of creative inquiry. This is where you let your imagination run wild. Allow your mind to wander, stray, and soar. Imagine a world in which the answers to your inquiries result in ground-breaking fixes or paradigm-shifting realizations.

Your creativity is allowed to run wild when you engage in imaginative exploration. Think of your questions as brushstrokes that add dimension and color to the canvas of possibilities that are in your mind. Let your ideas flow over the canvas, weaving a colorful tapestry of possibilities. This stage is about escaping the confines of traditional thought and having the courage to imagine a future in which creative solutions transform the world.

Through this approach, you are imagining a future that will be shaped by the force of your queries rather than merely daydreaming for the sake of fantasy. The combination of critical thinking and creativity is what takes you past the confines of the here and now and into a world where your knowledge may be used as a catalyst for good.

As you participate in this interactive exercise, remember that creativity and critical thinking are complementary rather than antagonistic. Similar to the two sides of a coin, they enhance one another's qualities and work in concert to raise your mental game. While imagination pushes you into the limitless regions of creativity and innovation, critical thinking anchors you in the world of logic and analysis.

Finding a balance between these two aspects enables you to skillfully negotiate the complex maze of ideas. It's not about choosing one over the other, but rather realizing how carefully critical analysis and creative discovery coexist. The secret to realizing your complete intellectual capacity is finding this balance.

Imagine it as a dance between the analytical and the creative, or as a symphony in which the melody is provided by imagination and the rhythm is defined by critical thinking. These components come together in your mind to create a work of intellectual discovery that is a masterwork.

Consider your tendencies as you immerse yourself in this challenge. How easily do you switch between analytical reasoning and creative exploration? Do you find that in your intellectual pursuits, one always takes precedence over the other, or do you find that they are seamlessly integrated?

Consider how this balance affects not just your view of the chosen issue but also your approach to problem-solving and brainstorming in other facets of your life. The abilities refined during this challenge go beyond the workout; they become instruments you employ in daily interactions, enhancing both your personal and professional pursuits.

The Interactive Challenge is a miniature version of the more extensive path of personal growth. It emphasizes how critical thinking and creative inquiry work well together and how their partnership can spark breakthrough ideas and ground-breaking discoveries.

After completing this challenge, pause to consider the journey. What insights did you gain regarding your thought processes? How did your investigation get shaped by the interaction of critical thinking and creativity? Keep these thoughts in mind as insightful observations about the dynamic interactions between your mental processes.

Recall that the mind is a large and complicated landscape that can be traversed with both inventiveness and accuracy while exploring the intricacies of thought. The Interactive Challenge turns into a figurative compass that leads you over the wide range of your cognitive talents. Accept this trip, for it holds the power to mold a future that reflects the inquisitiveness, ingenuity, and growth that are ingrained in your very nature.

One final thought:

Imagine stepping into a world that constantly tries to shape your thoughts, inundating you with a barrage of rules and laws governing everything from nature to the cosmos. Yet, as a budding critical thinker and visionary, this is your playground. To innovate, you must first delve into these guidelines, learning and understanding them not just to follow, but to creatively disrupt them. It's not about mere rebellion; it's about bending, twisting, and playing with the norms to forge something extraordinary.

Envision a world devoid of Einstein's daring challenge to the speed of light, or Picasso's defiance of artistic conventions. The greatest minds didn't just break rules; they rebuilt them into magnificent new realities. So, as you harness your critical thinking, analyze and deconstruct these rules. Let your imagination then take the reins, piecing them together into ideas that are not only groundbreaking but also uniquely yours. This journey of bending reality is not just an exercise in creativity, but a thrilling adventure that shapes the future. Embrace this power, and you'll be on the path to becoming one of the great minds who doesn't just follow the world but redefine it.

CHAPTER THREE
Developing Effective Relationships

Greetings, my dear reader, and welcome to a chapter that will attempt to untangle the complex web of creating a successful partnership. These pages act as a compass to help you navigate the transforming terrain where the strength of your relationships becomes the primary factor in your personal growth. We will explore the deep intersections of human contact in this investigation, learning how our growth story is shaped by relationships on both a personal and professional level.

Weaved throughout our lives, relationships have the power to act as catalysts for significant change. Remember that the keys to unlocking the infinite power found in connections are your natural curiosity and willingness to learn as we set out on our trip.

The deep understanding that we are social beings at our core is essential to healthy partnerships. The interactions that make up our lives are a tapestry of relationships, and the strength of these bonds has a profound impact on our overall well-being and personal growth. Our relationships act as mirrors, reflecting our beliefs, aspirations, and emotional landscapes, whether they are in the context of family, friendships, or professional networks.

Think about the fundamental nature of connection. It's not just about being close or having similar experiences; it's about the synergy that happens when people get to know, care for, and encourage one another. Let's start by dissecting the interpersonal dynamics that give productive relationships their depth and importance before delving into their specifics.

Effective communication is a basic component of relationship building. Think of communication as the links' lifeblood coursing through their veins. It is more than just speaking; it includes the capacity for thought and feeling as well as active listening and empathy. A culture of mutual trust and understanding is fostered by effective communication, which acts as a bridge to bridge gaps in understanding.

Consider your personal experiences. In what ways have instances of frank and transparent communication improved your relationships? How have you overcome obstacles with persuasive communication? When developed, communication is a talent that may be used to create and maintain strong relationships.

Another cornerstone of effective relationships is trust. Trust is the invisible thread that binds individuals, creating a sense of security and reliability. It's nurtured through consistency, transparency, and a genuine commitment to the well-being of those we connect with. Trust transforms relationships from superficial interactions into resilient bonds capable of withstanding the tests of time and adversity.

Think about the relationships in your life where mutual trust is essential. In what ways has trust enhanced these relationships? In what ways have you helped to create a trustworthy atmosphere? Once built, trust serves as the cornerstone around which successful relationships are built.

Another essential component of successful partnerships is empathy, which is commonly defined as the capacity to put oneself in another's shoes. It pushes us to truly comprehend and connect with the feelings and experiences of people around us, going beyond simple sympathy. Empathy fosters a sense of common humanity by establishing a connection that is beyond words.

Consider moments in your life when you felt fully understood and supported. What role did empathy play in the robustness of those connections? In what ways can you foster and demonstrate empathy in your relationships? Empathy becomes a useful tool for navigating the landscape of successful relationships since it points us in the direction of sincere connections.

Relationship give-and-take, or reciprocity, is a dynamic force that keeps ties from stagnating. It entails overcoming obstacles together in addition to celebrating victories and joys. Effective relationships are characterized by reciprocity that goes beyond simple transactions to include a continuous engagement in the development and welfare of both parties.

Consider the partnerships in which reciprocity has been a guiding principle. In what ways has the encouragement and support between the two parties improved such relationships? In what ways do you facilitate reciprocity in your relationships? As a principle, reciprocity ensures that healthy relationships are built on shared duties and experiences. It must be noted that reciprocity in relationships should never be forced or feel like an obligation. When that occurs, the friendship and relationship is suffering and devolving into something unhealthy.

Recognizing the variety of connections that influence our lives is crucial as we make our way through the maze of successful relationships. Whether friendly, familial, or professional, every relationship has its special dynamics and room for development. Accepting this diversity enables us to recognize the depth to which various relationships add to our personal growth.

Think about the different responsibilities you have in your life, such as those of a friend, mentor, coworker, or relative. What effects do these various responsibilities have on your growth? How can you take advantage of the particular dynamics in each relationship to advance both parties? Acknowledging and appreciating this difference becomes essential to the skill of building successful partnerships.

Let us now explore the importance of successful relationships in the framework of personal growth. Think of relationships as the soil in a garden that supports growth, and personal development as the plants. The health of the plants that emerge—your abilities, personality, and general well-being—is determined by the quality of this soil, which is enhanced by dialogue, trust, empathy, and reciprocity.

Consider how your relationships have influenced your growth. In what ways have encouraging relationships propelled your goals?

How have relationship difficulties helped you become more resilient and adaptable? Whether they are easy or difficult, relationships serve as the furnace in which the elements of personal growth are created.

Effective connections act as mirrors reflecting our areas of strength and growth when it comes to personal development. They provide comments, support, and occasionally helpful critique. We learn about our communication preferences, emotional intelligence, and teamwork abilities by negotiating the complexities of interpersonal relationships.

Think about the individuals in your life who have contributed significantly to your personal growth. In what ways have their viewpoints and comments influenced your path? In what ways have you helped people around you grow as a result? Good partnerships serve as mirrors, offering insightful reflections that direct us toward ongoing self-improvement.

In the workplace, having productive relationships is essential. They serve as the cornerstone for teamwork, creativity, and professional development. A workplace with these qualities— open communication, mutual trust, empathy for differing viewpoints, and reciprocal interactions—has limitless potential for growth and success.

Think back on your work-related experiences. What positive effects have connections had on your workplace? How have partnerships that foster collaboration helped initiatives reach new heights? The ability to establish productive relationships is a skill that is invaluable in the intricate fabric of the workplace.

Let's be honest as we work through this chapter on creating successful relationships: the process is never-ending. Similar to living things, relationships need ongoing maintenance, upkeep, and modification to thrive. Relationships stay vibrant and contribute to human development when individuals possess the capacity to learn from their interactions, modify their communication patterns, and cultivate trust and empathy.

Think of this chapter as a call to intentionally explore your relationships. How can you improve your partnerships' communication? How do you strengthen the reciprocity and trust in your network? In your encounters, how can you cultivate empathy? Accept these inquiries as seeds that, with care and planting, will become a garden of productive connections that enhance the rich terrain of your growth.

The Power of Teamwork

Welcome to a journey where you'll discover the incredible power of teamwork. You might think teamwork is just about groups working together, but it's so much more. It's like the secret ingredient that can make everything better in your life, from school projects to building friendships. So, buckle up, because together, we're going on an adventure of personal development through the magic of working together.

Think about the best team you've ever been a part of, whether it's a group project, a sports team, or just a bunch of friends playing games or hanging out. What made that team special? Was it how everyone supported each other or the amazing things you achieved together? Teamwork is like the secret sauce that takes ordinary groups and turns them into something extraordinary.

Picture this: You and your friends are planning a surprise party for a classmate. Each of you has a role, from organizing decorations to picking the perfect cake. The magic happens when you put all your ideas together and create something incredible. That's the power of teamwork.

Now, let's rewind for a moment. Have you ever been part of a group where things didn't quite click? Maybe there was a miscommunication, and people felt left out or frustrated. That's when teamwork didn't work its magic. But don't worry; we'll explore how to make sure that doesn't happen.

So, why is teamwork important? How does it relate to your personal development? The answer is simple: working together teaches you valuable life skills. It's like a training ground for communication, problem-solving, and understanding others. The more you embrace teamwork, the more you grow as an individual.

Now that we've opened the door to the world of teamwork, let's talk about your teamwork toolbox. Think of it as your trusty backpack filled with skills and strategies to make every team experience amazing.

Consider this scenario: You're working on a school project with classmates. You notice that some team members have fantastic ideas, while others are great at organizing and keeping everyone on track. Your critical thinking skills come into play as you identify everyone's strengths and figure out how to put them together like pieces of a puzzle.

Take a moment to reflect: How often do you think about your role in a team? Do you actively seek ways to contribute your strengths, whether it's leadership, creativity, or organization? Your willingness to embrace balanced complexity enriches your teamwork experiences.

Teamwork is like a puzzle. Each person brings unique pieces to the table, and when you put them together, you create something amazing. Just as a puzzle becomes more captivating as you fit the pieces, teamwork becomes more rewarding as you understand and appreciate each team member's strengths.

Imagine this: Your team faces a challenge, like completing a complex project with a tight deadline. Your ability to think critically and find solutions becomes your team's compass. You navigate the bumps in the road, adapt to changes, and keep everyone focused on the end goal.

Now, think about the art of storytelling. When an author crafts a thrilling story, they weave together different characters, each with their strengths and weaknesses. Similarly, in a team, you're like characters in a story. Your diverse talents and personalities create a narrative of growth and accomplishment.

Let's dive into a thought-provoking question: How often do you consciously observe your teamwork dynamics? How do you adapt when challenges arise? How do empathy and understanding play a role in successful teamwork? By inviting critical thinking and empathy into your team interactions, you're setting the stage for remarkable achievements.

Empowerment is like the treasure you find on this teamwork adventure. It's about discovering your strengths, gaining confidence, and knowing that you can achieve incredible things as part of a team. By cultivating your teamwork skills, you empower yourself to tackle challenges and make a real difference.

Imagine your life as a dynamic playing field, and you, an essential player in the game of personal development. In this expansive arena, the concept of teamwork emerges as a parallel to a sports team striving for victory. Each player, with a distinct role, contributes to the collective pursuit of success. As you navigate this field, you find yourself part of various teams—be it in the workplace, within your social circles, or even in your family. These teams become the training grounds where the skills of effective communication, mutual support, and shared celebrations are honed.

Think about your role in these diverse teams. How do you harness your strengths to empower yourself and others? What strategies can you employ to elevate the collaborative spirit within the team? The journey toward personal development, much like a sports team aiming for victory, demands both active participation and reflective contemplation.

Consider the synergy of communication within a sports team. In the heat of the game, players communicate swiftly and effectively, passing critical information to ensure seamless coordination. Similarly, in your life's pursuits, effective communication becomes the linchpin of successful teamwork. It involves not only conveying your thoughts clearly but also actively listening to the perspectives of others. By fostering an environment of open and honest communication, you contribute to the team's collective intelligence and problem-solving capabilities.

Reflect on instances where communication played a pivotal role in a team effort. How did the clarity of communication influence the team's performance? How did active listening enhance the team's ability to adapt to challenges? As you contemplate these experiences, recognize the impact of communication in shaping the dynamics of effective teamwork.

Now, let's delve into the concept of support within a team. In a sports team, players rally around each other, offering encouragement during challenging moments and celebrating victories together. This camaraderie strengthens the team's unity and resilience. In your personal development journey, the principle of mutual support holds equal significance. Your ability to uplift others and seek support when needed creates a collaborative atmosphere that fosters growth.

Think about a time when the support of your team was instrumental in overcoming a challenge. How did the collective encouragement impact your motivation and determination? How can you, in turn, provide support to others within your teams? Recognizing the symbiotic nature of support within teams unveils the transformative potential embedded in shared victories and shared struggles.

Celebrating victories, irrespective of their size, is an integral part of team dynamics. In sports, a team rejoices in every goal scored, recognizing that each small triumph contributes to the overall success. Apply this principle to your personal development journey. Acknowledge and celebrate your achievements, no matter how modest, and extend this celebration to the achievements of your team members. By collectively reveling in accomplishments, you create a positive feedback loop that fuels motivation and inspires continuous improvement.

Reflect on the significance of celebrating victories within your teams. How does the acknowledgment of achievements contribute to the team's morale? How can you cultivate a culture of celebration within your personal and professional circles? As you ponder these questions, grasp the notion that shared celebrations amplify the sense of accomplishment, reinforcing the team's commitment to shared goals.

Now, as we navigate deeper into this exploration of teamwork, consider your role as both a player and a leader within the various teams you belong to. In a sports team, leaders emerge not just from designated roles but from individuals who inspire and guide their teammates. Similarly, in your life, leadership within a team involves fostering a positive and collaborative environment.

Think about the leaders who have inspired you within your teams. What qualities did they possess that motivated and guided the team toward success? How can you embody these leadership qualities within your roles? Recognizing the transformative potential of leadership within teams empowers you to contribute actively to the team's synergy and development.

The Adventure Begins: Embrace the Magic of Teamwork

Set off on a trip filled with the magic of teamwork, where the spirit of the group rises above simple cooperation to reach new heights of mutual development, individual progress, and the fulfillment of dreams that previously seemed unattainable.

Think about the idea that working as a team is a journey of mutual progress rather than just a regimented ballet of chores. It's a dynamic process that moves people to become better versions of themselves, each step taking place in unison with the others to make a collective ascension.

As you embark on this captivating journey, picture a team as a community dedicated to mutual growth rather than just a collection of people working side by side. Imagine a team's identity as a dynamic mosaic created by the varied talents that are woven together like a tapestry. Through this cooperative endeavor, the voyage turns into a trigger for individual and group metamorphosis.

The pursuit of common objectives by all members of the team is the essence of collaboration. It's about lining up personal goals with group aims and creating a story in which each person's path is intertwined around a shared goal. Through this collaborative effort, people learn that the team is a synergistic entity capable of accomplishing achievements beyond individual imaginations, not merely the sum of its parts.

Let's now discuss the idea of growth in the context of teamwork. See every member of the team as a distinct seed planted in the rich soil of teamwork. Individual seeds grow into plants of both individual and group development as the team prospers. The sharing of successes, the flow of ideas, and the teamwork combine to create a fertile environment in which each individual grows.

Think back to times in your own life when personal development has been accelerated by teamwork. How have you changed as a person in the ever-changing environment of a team? What personal growth opportunities have you had as a result of the group journey? Acknowledging these turning points reveals the captivating enchantment that occurs when people come together on a road of mutual advancement.

In addition to enhancing individual abilities, teamwork fosters flexibility and resilience. Consider the team as a dynamic ecosystem in which impediments don't stand in the way of learning as a group. Through the ups and downs of teamwork, people learn to be resilient to setbacks and versatile enough to flourish in a variety of settings.

Think about the comparison of a team working on a difficult project. The difficulties faced become stepping stones rather than barriers, each strengthening the team's fortitude. The team's DNA is altered to include the capacity to overcome obstacles, come up with creative solutions, and adjust to changing conditions. This makes the team an unstoppable force that can overcome any obstacle.

Think about the adaptability and resilience that you have developed in the face of adversity as you consider your experiences working in teams. How have these group activities changed obstacles into opportunities for development? How has the fluidity of teamwork given you the ability to adapt to the always-shifting terrain of joint ventures?

The intangible relationship that arises among individuals is the source of the enchantment of teamwork, surpassing even physical results. Imagine the team spirit as a force that cuts beyond the ordinary and creates bonds that have a deeper meaning. Team members are woven together in a web of trust by their tacit understanding, mutual support during setbacks, and shared joy in times of success.

Consider an instance where a team's synergy turned a difficult circumstance into a shared success. In what ways did the common experiences foster ties of trust and friendship? How does the unseen power of teamwork improve each team member's trip as a whole? Acknowledging these relationships' strengths raises the importance of teamwork above and beyond assignments and projects.

There is an alchemy in the magic of teamwork that turns individuals into a cohesive force that can accomplish things that are beyond the reach of individual endeavors. As you embark on this captivating journey, remember that the team and the individual are mutually dependent. The individual helps the team evolve as a whole while the team offers a supportive atmosphere for personal development.

Consider your personal experience working in teams. What personal contributions have you made to the development and success of the team? In what ways has the team as a whole facilitated your personal growth? Acknowledging this mutual swaying between the person and the group reveals the subtle nuances of enchantment innate in the cooperative mindset.

As the adventure unfolds, remember that the magic of teamwork isn't confined to specific tasks or projects. It permeates the essence of personal and collective development, transforming the ordinary into the extraordinary. It's about growing together, becoming better versions of ourselves, and achieving heights beyond our wildest dreams. With every collaborative step, the magic of teamwork weaves its spell, creating a tapestry where individual and collective aspirations harmonize in the symphony of shared achievement.

Hey, future team leader! Think about the incredible power of teamwork. It's not just a group effort, it's about creating magic together. Remember, a "team" can be as small as two minds united by trust and passion. History is filled with dynamic duos who changed the game, like the astronauts of Apollo 11 or the scientists Watson and Crick.

Teamwork is about amplifying possibilities, not just dividing tasks. When you collaborate, you can achieve bigger goals, reach higher dreams, and celebrate greater victories. Imagine being co-pilots, not competitors, each flying high on the other's strengths.

What kind of teammate do you want to be? Be the one who uplifts in tough times, offers wisdom amidst chaos, and extends a helping hand when needed. Your positive energy can transform individual efforts into a unified force, inspiring the whole team.

In a team, accountability is your safety net, ensuring no one faces challenges alone. Your support can be a lifeline for a teammate in need. Embracing everyone's unique skills is key to fairness in a team. Maybe you're great at strategizing while your friend excels in logistics – together, you're unstoppable.

View your teammate as your ally in an exciting journey. Teamwork isn't just a luxury, it's the foundation of lasting friendships and successful endeavors. Be the supportive sidekick in your team's story, not overshadowing but amplifying each other's strengths.

Remember, teamwork goes beyond achieving goals. It's about forging lasting bonds. The challenges and victories you share build a tapestry of trust and memories. These experiences are invaluable. So invest in your team, build bridges of understanding and respect. After all, the bonds formed through teamwork are the real triumphs. Ready to embrace the power of teamwork? The world awaits your combined magic!

The Superpower of Empathy

Welcome to the realm of empathy, a superpower that not only enriches your development journey but also weaves a profound connection with the world around you. It's like having a magic key that opens the door to understanding, compassion, and meaningful relationships.

A key competency that promotes successful communication, teamwork, and healthy relationships is conflict resolution. Let's examine several actions and strategies for effectively resolving conflicts:

1. Define the Issue: Begin by clearly defining the specific issue or problem causing the conflict. Identify the root cause, as conflicts often arise from misunderstandings or differing perspectives.

2. Active Listening: Actively listen to the concerns, perspectives, and emotions of all parties involved. Listening attentively fosters understanding and demonstrates respect for each person's viewpoint.

3. Empathize: Put yourself in the shoes of others to understand their feelings and motivations. Empathy creates a bridge of understanding, acknowledging the emotional aspect of the conflict.

4. Stay Calm: Maintain emotional control and avoid reacting or speaking impulsively. Calmness contributes to a more constructive environment for resolving conflicts.

5. Encourage Open Communication: Create a safe space for open and honest communication. Encourage all parties to express their thoughts and feelings without fear of judgment.

6. Find Common Ground: Identify areas of agreement or common goals. Establishing common ground helps build a foundation for collaboration and resolution.

7. Seek Solutions, Not Blame: Shift the focus from assigning blame to finding solutions. Collaborate on identifying mutually beneficial outcomes that address the concerns of all parties.

8. Brainstorm Solutions: Engage in a collaborative brainstorming session to generate potential solutions. Encourage creativity and explore various options to address the conflict.

9. Evaluate Pros and Cons: Assess the potential solutions by evaluating their pros and cons. Consider the long-term impact and feasibility of each option. Think about "The Law of Unintended Consequences".

10. Negotiate: Engage in a negotiation process to reach a compromise. Flexibility and a willingness to meet in the middle contribute to successful conflict resolution.

11. Establish Clear Agreements: Clearly define the agreed-upon solutions and expectations. Establishing clear agreements helps prevent future misunderstandings.

12. Follow Up: Periodically follow up on the resolution to ensure that the agreed-upon solutions are implemented and effective.

This demonstrates commitment to maintaining positive outcomes.

13. Involve a Third Party: In situations where resolution is challenging, consider involving a neutral third party, such as a teacher, parent, mediator, or arbitrator, to facilitate the process.

14. Provide Feedback: Constructive feedback is essential for continuous improvement. Share feedback on the conflict resolution process and explore ways to enhance future interactions.

15. Learn and Adapt: Treat conflicts as learning opportunities. Reflect on the resolution process and apply lessons learned to improve conflict management skills in the future.

Recall that disagreements arise frequently in interpersonal relationships and that finding common ground, being patient, and being actively involved are all necessary for successful conflict resolution. Through the application of these strategies and actions, both individuals and groups can effectively manage disagreements and cultivate more robust connections.

Let's embark on a reflective exploration by delving into the intriguing question: Have you ever experienced that uncanny ability to comprehend someone's feelings without a single word being spoken? It's the marvel of empathy in action, akin to wearing a special pair of glasses that grants you the ability to see the world through another person's eyes.

Imagine a scenario where you're sitting with a friend who appears distressed. Though they remain silent, your intuitive empathy kicks in, nudging your curiosity to gently inquire if they wish to share. In that moment, by being present and actively listening, you've demonstrated the essence of empathy. It's not about having all the answers; it's about creating a space for understanding and connection.

Now, let's rewind to moments in your life when you longed for someone to grasp the depth of your emotions. Perhaps it was the anxiety before a test or the weight of a challenging day at school. This is where empathy transforms into a bridge, linking individuals through shared experiences and emotions. It becomes a conduit for genuine connection, fostering understanding and support.

So, why is empathy a cornerstone of personal development? How does it contribute to your growth as an individual? The answer lies in the simplicity of empathy serving as a key that unlocks the gates to meaningful relationships. It enables you to comprehend others on a profound level, navigate conflicts with sensitivity, and offer support when it's most needed. Embracing empathy becomes a catalyst for your evolution.

Now that we've opened the door to the world of empathy, let's delve into your empathy toolkit—an invaluable treasure chest filled with skills and strategies to infuse every interaction with compassion and understanding.

Active Listening: Imagine your empathy toolkit as a well-crafted instrument, and active listening as its melodious tune. When engaging with others, listen not just to respond but to understand. Consider for a moment how often someone is speaking, and you get very excited to share your input. Were you actively listening or just responding? Tune in to both verbal and non-verbal cues and let the symphony of empathy play.

Cultivating Curiosity: Curiosity is the fuel that propels your empathy engine. Be genuinely interested in others' perspectives, experiences, and emotions. Ask open-ended questions that invite them to share their stories, creating a space for mutual understanding. Avoid yes or no questions when possible.

Practicing Perspective-Taking: Empathy thrives when you can step into someone else's shoes. Imagine perspective-taking as a lens in your toolkit that allows you to view the world from different angles. It broadens your understanding and nurtures empathy. Step back and think about an unpleasant situation a friend experienced. Now consider how experiencing that situation would impact your life.

Expressing Empathy Through Body Language: The body speaks a language of its own. Your toolkit includes the ability to convey empathy through non-verbal cues—maintaining eye contact, offering a comforting touch, or mirroring emotions. These gestures amplify the impact of your empathy.

Cultivating Emotional Intelligence: Picture emotional intelligence as the compass in your toolkit that guides your empathetic journey. Develop a keen awareness of your own emotions and those of others. Understand how emotions influence behavior, fostering deeper connections.

Acknowledging and Validating Feelings: Your toolkit is equipped with the power to acknowledge and validate others' feelings. Whether it's joy, sorrow, or frustration, recognizing and respecting their emotions strengthens the bonds of empathy.

Empathy in Action: Transform your empathy from a passive concept into an active force. Engage in acts of kindness, offer a listening ear, or extend a helping hand. Empathy, when translated into action, becomes a dynamic force for positive change.

As you explore and hone the skills within your empathy toolkit, envision each interaction as an opportunity to create ripples of understanding and connection. Your journey with empathy is not just a personal odyssey but a collective venture, weaving a tapestry of shared emotions, compassion, and growth. So, open your empathy toolkit with curiosity and compassion, and let the magic of understanding unfold in every interaction on your personal development journey.

Think of empathy like a puzzle, with each person you meet having a different set of parts. You have the chance to piece together the unique experiences, feelings, and thoughts that make up each individual. Your role is to attentively listen, keenly observe, and piece together their tale. The more you invest in understanding others, the more complete and intricate the picture becomes. In this sense, empathy serves as the link between the various facets of the human experience.

Imagine that you have a friend who is very excitedly telling you how much they love a new book that is in a genre you might not normally read. However, you can put yourself in their position and feel their excitement by developing empathy. Even if your hobbies are different, empathy serves as a bridge that lets you connect with their feelings. It turns an ordinary talk into a happy moment spent together. This capacity to emotionally connect with people strengthens relationships and creates a feeling of shared experience.

Here's a provocative question for you to consider: How often do you intentionally practice empathy in your daily interactions? Consider how the dynamics of your relationships with friends, family, and even strangers are altered by this deliberate act. Being empathetic is more than just being passive; it's being involved in the world. Deeper connections and a more complex comprehension of the human condition are made possible by fusing critical thinking and empathy.

Gaining mastery over the superpower of empathy leads to empowerment. It's about appreciating the great impact you can have on the world by genuinely understanding and helping others around you; it goes beyond simply understanding others. By developing your empathy, you give yourself the ability to help make the world a more peaceful and caring place. It's the realization that your capacity to deeply connect with people may be a catalyst for good in the world.

Consider empathy as a cascading impact. Empathy has an impact that goes beyond the person you are extending it to. Being empathetic and understanding spreads like wildfire, encouraging others to do the same. Like throwing a pebble into a pond, it creates ripples that extend far beyond the original site of contact. As a result, every tiny act of empathy has the power to start a kindness chain reaction, building a powerful wave of positive effects.

Consider your place in this superpower of empathy. How do you actively engage in empathetic behavior daily? What techniques can you use to improve your empathy and comprehension? Realize that empathy is a superpower with the capacity to change both your life and the lives of those around you. It is not only a talent that has to be developed. When you practice empathy, you start to weave meaningful connections and become a constructive force in the complex web of human relationships.

CHAPTER FOUR
Managing Time and Responsibilities

Greetings and welcome to the fascinating quest that most of us start at a young age: learning to manage our time and obligations. We'll untangle the complex web that exists between education, extracurriculars, family time, and personal development in these pages. Hold on, this isn't your average lecture; rather, it's an examination and an opportunity for you to consider how you might prioritize your development while navigating the complex web of duties.

Imagine this: The steady chime of your alarm clock announces the start of your day, and then—bam! Time is of the essence in this race. It's difficult to juggle school, schoolwork, sports practice, and chores at the same time. Are you able to relate? If so, you are not alone. For many teenagers, including yourself, time management is a daily conundrum.

Let me now throw this idea your way: How frequently do you take a moment to evaluate how well you manage your time? Does it sometimes sound like a disorganized cacophony or is it a masterfully planned symphony of productivity? To become proficient in this art, one must not only complete duties but also exercise critical thinking and self-awareness.

As you read through this chapter, picture your day as a blank canvas just waiting for your creative input. Every duty represents a hue on your color scheme, and you know what? The artist is you. Making a perfect masterpiece is not the point; the purpose is to plan a day that supports your personal growth objectives.

Let's not forget that life is unpredictable, nevertheless. Unexpected turns, such as an unexpected invitation or pop quiz, may occur. That's where balance and adaptation are useful. It's about accepting change and maintaining your focus on your objectives.

Now how can I possibly balance everything and still have time for myself?" you may be asking yourself. That's when prioritization and time management skills become magical. It all comes down to prioritizing your priorities and managing your time effectively.

A hint of well-balanced complexity is this: Time management involves more than just crossing things off your to-do list; it also involves knowing your values, establishing objectives, and making deliberate decisions. It involves planning a timetable that is both effective and significant, leaving time for leisure, interests, and personal development.

Recall that this is an exploratory trip. You'll try out various tactics, figure out what suits you, and adjust as you go. Consider your life as a continuous project in which you play the roles of protagonist, manager, and creative director.

Let's talk tech while we work through this intricacy together. What effects do social media, apps, and cell phones have on your day-to-day activities and time management? Consider how you can use these tools to your advantage while preserving a sensible equilibrium.

Let's get started on our personal development now. It's about being the best version of yourself, not just about handling obligations. Think of it like a puzzle, where each responsibility piece fits into the overall design that represents your personal development.

Amidst the complex issues of personal growth and time management, never forget that you are not traveling alone. Like you, a lot of teenagers are attempting to find balance, manage the complexities of their duties, and advance personally. It's a common experience, and people may relate to your struggles and accomplishments.

I would like to share a parting view to help bring things into focus. If you were to calculate the average amount of time spent on random activities for a typical teenager in today's world and write them out, you might find yourself in awe at how you can sometimes get so much done. Check these numbers out.

1. School (6-8 hours): This chunk of your day is packed with classes, labs, and school activities. It's where you dive into various subjects and participate in engaging discussions.

2. Meals & Breaks (1-2 hours): These are crucial times for refueling and relaxing. Whether it's lunchtime, snack breaks, or just a moment to chill, use these breaks wisely to recharge.

3. Homework & Studying (1-3 hours): Tackling assignments, preparing for tests, and doing research is vital. This is your time to solidify what you learned in school and get ahead.

4. Chores & Errands (30-60 minutes): From cleaning up around the house to running errands, these tasks are part of daily life. They might seem small, but they add up in terms of responsibility.

5. Commute & Getting Ready (30-60 minutes): Traveling to school and getting ready in the morning are parts of your routine that you can streamline for efficiency.

6. Personal Hygiene (20-30 minutes): Taking care of yourself, like showering and brushing your teeth, is non-negotiable. Good hygiene is good health.

7. Interruptions & Distractions (1-2 hours): Here's the tricky part – the distractions. Social media, daydreaming, or unplanned chats can eat into your productivity. Be mindful of these time-stealers.

8. Entertainment (2-5 hours): Everyone needs downtime. Gaming, watching shows, or hanging out with friends are great, but balance is key.

Time Summation

Productive Time : School, homework, chores, and personal hygiene can take up about 8.5 to 14 hours of your day.

Distracted Time : Those sneaky distractions? They can take up 1-2 hours.

Unproductive Time : Entertainment, while fun, can amount to 2-5 hours.

Scenario Calculations

1. Full Day (All Activities): If you do everything, starting at 7 AM, you might not finish until midnight – that's a 17-hour day!
2. Essentials + Interruptions: Skipping just the unproductive entertainment, your day might end around 10:30 PM. Still a solid 15.5 hours.
3. Only Must-Dos: Focusing purely on essentials and cutting out distractions and entertainment? You could be all done by 9:30 PM – 14.5 hours.

Seeing it all laid out like this, it's clear how quickly time can slip away. The key is critical thinking about your day and planning for success. Recognize where your time goes and make conscious decisions about how to spend it. Maybe it's setting specific times for social media or gaming, or maybe it's finding more efficient ways to tackle chores and errands. Remember, every minute you manage well today is an investment in your tomorrow. With a bit of planning and some smart choices, you can strike the perfect balance between work and play, making the most of every hour in your day. You've got this!

Time Management: Harnessing Moments

Greetings, young time traveler. Yes, you heard that right - you're about to embark on a journey through the fascinating realm of time management. While you won't be jumping through centuries, you'll learn how to make the most of every moment in your life. So, buckle up, and let's harness those moments together.

Do you know that the ability to effectively manage time and obligations is not limited by age or profession? Our daily lives are a complicated fabric made of choices, priorities, and flexibility, all of which work together in harmony. We will explore the fundamentals of efficient time management and the skill of deftly balancing obligations in our inquiry.

A basic query that sits at the center of our adventure is: How can we maximize our time while attending to all of our obligations? The answer is a customized strategy that takes into account each person's values, goals, and the dynamic nature of life rather than a one-size-fits-all solution. Let's break out the components of time management first. Essentially, time management is a comprehensive approach to maximizing the use of our most valuable resource—not just packing more work into each day. It entails prioritizing things, creating objectives, and making deliberate decisions that are consistent with our values.

Imagine your day as a canvas waiting to be painted. Each responsibility represents a stroke of color, contributing to the vibrant masterpiece of your life. The challenge is not in eliminating the colors but in blending them harmoniously, creating a fabric that reflects your unique journey.

One crucial aspect of effective time management is self-awareness. How often do you pause to reflect on how you spend your time? It's easy to get caught up in the whirlwind of tasks and obligations, losing sight of the bigger picture. Taking a step back allows us to assess our priorities, identify time-wasting habits, and make conscious decisions about where our time should be invested.

Picture this: Your alarm clock begins to gently chime as you awaken. There is yet another day ahead of us, full of obligations and chores. The schedule is full of classes, homework, extracurricular activities, and personal leisure. The truth is, time is the great equalizer, my inquisitive friend. We have 24 hours in a day, no more, no less. Your ability to handle these hours will determine how successful you are.

You're probably already an expert at managing your time. You've probably balanced your hobbies, schoolwork, and socializing with pals. The essential query, though, is this: How can you use time management to further your personal growth? How can you make each second of the clock matter?

Now let's be contemplative for a bit. Have you ever wondered how some people manage to get so much done in a day that seems so short to you? It's not a secret ability or a magic trick. Time management is a skill that can be learned by anyone prepared to put in the necessary effort.

Consider this: You are the captain of a ship sailing over the great ocean of time. Your aspirations and goals are your destinations. You'll need a map and a well-calibrated compass to go to them. Time management can help with that; it's like a compass, and your goals are like the North Star.

There's a catch, though: life isn't a straightforward journey. Unexpected occurrences, or storms, may come your way, and you may need to change your course at times. That's why flexibility is so important. Effective time management involves navigating life's uncertainties with grace rather than following an inflexible timetable.

Effective time management involves more than just fitting chores into your schedule like puzzle pieces. It's a mindful craft that calls for planning, prioritization, and introspection about your personal priorities. Finding a perfect balance between your obligations and your desires is key.

This is where the role of curiosity comes in. How can you investigate time management strategies that personally appeal to you? Do you think using digital tools like to-do lists and calendars would be beneficial, or do you think using planners and sticky notes is a more tactile method? You have the option.

Effective time management involves more than just completing things; it also involves allowing yourself the flexibility and room you need to thrive. Consider it like taking care of a garden: you need to make sure the soil is conducive to new growth (your personal development) as well as water the flowers, which represents your duties.

Not all time management exercises need to be serious affairs. You may even tinker with it and add originality to it. Convert assignments into challenges, measure your performance against your records, and acknowledge and appreciate your progress.

While we maneuver through this complex dance, it is impossible to overlook the role that technology plays in this dance. Social media, applications, and smartphones have ingrained themselves into our everyday lives, changing the way we work, interact, and unwind. Although these gadgets provide never-before-seen convenience, there's a chance they could end up being time-consuming distractions. The secret is to use technology to our advantage and to make it a helper, not a barrier, in efficient time management.

Let's now explore the topic of responsibility. Academic, professional, familial, and personal are some of the forms they take. It takes dexterity to strike a balance between these many obligations; it's like doing a high-wire act where balance and accuracy are crucial. Every duty has importance and adds to the broader framework of our existence.

The secret to efficient time management and prioritization is understanding what is most important to us. It involves distinguishing between critical and urgent jobs, comprehending our long-term objectives, and scheduling our time appropriately. In order to make sure that our everyday actions are in line with our larger goals, this process entails a continuous assessment of our values.

When you consider your day as an investment portfolio, where time is your most valuable currency, each activity or choice becomes a critical investment decision. Just like in financial portfolios, the goal is to maximize returns – in this case, your personal development, happiness, and overall well-being. But there's more to it. Just as with financial investments, there are risks involved. Making a bad investment with your time can not only hinder the growth of your 'portfolio', but it can also set back what you've already achieved.

For instance, spending excessive time on activities with little to no return – like aimless internet browsing or unproductive daydreaming – is akin to investing in a declining stock. It depletes your valuable time without offering any real benefits, leading to missed opportunities for growth. Moreover, poor time investments can create negative habits, draining your energy and focus, which are crucial assets in your daily life.

On the flip side, investing your time in productive and fulfilling activities is like putting your money into high-growth stocks or stable, reliable assets. These activities not only provide immediate satisfaction and development but also compound over time, leading to greater personal growth and well-being. This could mean dedicating time to learn a new skill, focusing on physical fitness, or nurturing meaningful relationships.

Therefore, just like a savvy investor, you need to be strategic and thoughtful about where you allocate your time. Assess the 'return on investment' of your daily activities. Are they contributing positively to your life goals? Are they enhancing your knowledge, health, or happiness? Being mindful of the potential gains and losses, and adjusting your 'investment strategy' accordingly, is crucial in maximizing the value of your time. By doing so, you can ensure that your day yields the best possible returns in personal growth and satisfaction.

In the pursuit of effective time management, the concept of a balanced life emerges. It's not about overloading yourself with tasks or succumbing to the pressure of external expectations. Instead, it's a nuanced dance where you allocate time not just for work but also for personal growth, hobbies, and moments of relaxation. The goal is not to merely survive each day but to thrive in a life that encompasses diverse experiences and pursuits.

As we navigate this landscape, adaptability becomes a crucial skill. Life is inherently unpredictable, throwing unexpected challenges and opportunities our way. The ability to adapt, to pivot our plans without losing sight of our goals, is a hallmark of effective time management. It's about embracing change rather than resisting it, recognizing that flexibility is the key to navigating the ebb and flow of life.

Let's now turn our attention to the interdisciplinary process of personal growth. Effective time management is an essential part of the bigger picture of being the best versions of ourselves, not a stand-alone concept. Every duty and hour prudently spent adds to our development pattern.

Consider personal growth as an ongoing process of evolution instead of a final destination. It entails learning about oneself, developing new skills, and cultivating a resilient, learning-oriented attitude. Our responsibilities are like steppingstones that help us move forward on this path of transformation.

As you explore the multifaceted themes of time management and personal development, remember that you're not alone on this journey. Many people, young and old, just like you are striving to make every moment count, to steer their ships toward their dreams, and to discover the hidden treasures of time.

Organizational Skills: Order in Chaos

Greetings, readers, from the world of ordered chaos! You will discover how to apply the power of order in the middle of the turmoil of your busy life as we delve into the fascinating world of organizing abilities in this chapter. Thus, buckle up, for we are about to set out on an exciting voyage of discovery!

Take a moment to consider your life. You're surrounded by a frenzy of obligations and activities, including school, schoolwork, extracurricular activities, friendships, and a little bit of personal time. You now have a concoction of possible mayhem when you add a dash of adolescent impulsivity. But fear not—we are here to guide you through it.

It can frequently feel like a tumultuous rollercoaster navigating the maelstrom of assignments, deadlines, and responsibilities that come with being a teenager or young adult. But hidden within the mayhem is a weapon that can change your life daily: organizing abilities. See it as the magic wand that helps you navigate the rollercoaster with efficiency and grace by bringing order to the chaos.

First, let's admit that there is chaos. You have a lot on your plate in terms of schoolwork, extracurricular activities, social obligations, and finding time for personal development and self-care. Even the most seasoned circus performer would be surprised by this juggling trick.

So, the question is, how can you make your way through this chaotic environment and come out not just alive but also prospering? In the turbulent terrain of adolescence, chaos takes on a familiar role. As schoolwork mounts, extracurricular activities take up more time on the schedule, and social commitments appear one after the other, the noise of responsibilities grows louder. Even the most skilled multitasker may feel like they're walking a tightrope without a safety net due to the kaleidoscope of demands. Finding time for self-care and personal development is a critical component that frequently gets overlooked in the midst of this chaos.

The sheer amount and diversity of duties resemble a juggling act, a sophisticated show in which every ball stands for a distinct aspect of life, including social, personal, extracurricular, and academic. Imagine yourself throwing schoolwork into the air, attempting to catch the fast-moving clubs of extracurricular activities, and delicately balancing the elaborately patterned balls of social obligations. A seasoned circus performer would be impressed by this show and would raise an eyebrow.

Teenage life seems to be meant to test your fortitude, your ability to maintain concentration in the face of chaos, and your ability to not only survive but thrive. It's a furnace where developing organizational abilities, flexibility, and time management are key components.

The pursuit of personal development and self-care frequently fades into the background in this whirling storm, like a flimsy hope amid the mayhem. But it's at these chaotic times that resilience and self-discovery can sprout like a flower. Then, the poignant question arises: How can one not just survive but thrive in this seemingly chaotic landscape?

The key is to view the mayhem as a necessary component of living and an opportunity for personal development rather than an overwhelming obstacle. It entails realizing the various demands on your time and energy and realizing how each task fits into the larger picture of your life.

Think of the turmoil as a blank canvas just ready for your own artistic touches. Every duty and every commitment are a color that enhances the richness and vitality of the work of art you are making. It's not about getting rid of the chaos; rather, it's about learning to dance in it and discover a beat that suits your ambitions.

Let's now explore the tactics that can turn the turmoil into a power source. It starts with accepting chaos as a traveling companion rather than an enemy. Recognize that the maelstrom of duties is a chance to improve your capacity to manage your time, acquire the fine art of setting priorities, and realize the value of flexibility.

Think of time management as your go-to tool—a compass that helps you navigate the maze of responsibilities. Make a schedule that allows you to balance your enjoyment of your hobbies with the responsibilities of your studies. Larger jobs can be broken down into smaller, more manageable pieces, which can help you move through the turmoil with direction and purpose. As old the saying goes, how do you eat an elephant? One bite at a time.

Your organizational abilities will help you navigate the storm of tasks. Fundamentally, these abilities are about setting up procedures and systems that let you efficiently manage your time and resources. These are the instruments by which you conquer disorder and restore some kind of regularity to your life. As you progress, prioritization will become your ally. Certain tasks are more important than others and will have a greater impact on your overall development. Determine which tasks are most important to you and give them the attention they require.

Organizational skills, which are sometimes disregarded during chaos, will become your architects of order. You will clear your mental and physical space to create a space that is conducive to creativity and focus. You will create systems and routines that will turn the chaos into a well-choreographed dance, with each step intentional and meaningful.

Adaptability turns into a powerful asset. Because life is unpredictable by nature, teenage upheaval is not an exception. Accept change as a chance for improvement and a chance to hone your tactics. The capacity to turn tactfully when faced with unforeseen turns guarantees that the mayhem won't stop you from moving forward but rather accelerate it.

You see, developing organizational skills isn't about turning into a tidy freak or making calendars that are meticulously color-coded (though if that's your thing, by all means, do it!). Instead, it's about discovering your rhythm within your life's symphony. It's about writing a song that enables you to balance your obligations and your interests.

So, allow me to be critical for a bit. Have you ever wondered how certain people manage to cross tasks off their to-do lists with elegance and ease as they go through life? It's a skill, my inquisitive friend; it's not magic. It's the capacity to control the chaos and impose order on your surroundings so that they serve you rather than work against you.

Imagine this: On a school day, you wake up and go about your morning routine with ease, rather than frantically looking for your schoolwork or your lost phone. Your daily duties are all well-organized, your backpack is prepared, and you even have time for a quick self-care break. What is the sound of that? Realistic? Indeed.

Developing organizational abilities involves clearing your mind as much as organizing your physical surroundings. It involves clearing a mental space where you can think, analyze ideas critically, and make judgments free from distracting thoughts.

This is where the role of personal development comes in. Like the soil in which you sow the seeds of your growth, organizational abilities are essential. Effective time and possession management creates mental room for you to discover new passions, pick up new abilities, and grow into the greatest version of yourself.

Organizing your life doesn't have to be all seriousness and no fun. Turn it into a game, challenge yourself to beat your records, and reward yourself for hitting your organizational goals. The journey to order can be as enjoyable as the destination.

Essentially, managing the turmoil of adolescence is a skill that requires juggling obligations, developing fortitude, and discovering happy and self-revealing moments within the confusion. It's about realizing that chaos can be used to create a lively, meaningful, and distinctively you rather than as a barrier. Thus, while you move through this complex dance, accept the confusion, create your masterpiece, and let the adventure play out with fortitude, direction, and a hint of magic mixed with chaos.

As we navigate the complexity of organizational skills, remember that you're not alone in this adventure. Many teens like you are seeking the magic formula to balance their lives and discover the serenity within order. It's a journey, not a destination, and you're equipped with the tools to make it a success.

Stress Management

Ah, the thrilling highs, thrilling lows, and unexpected loop-de-loops that life throws at you—the rollercoaster ride of youth. Let's dive into the enigmatic world of stress management as we begin the last section of this chapter. Stress management is an essential ability for any young mind navigating the turbulent terrain of adolescence and early adulthood.

Stress is an unavoidable aspect of life and a continuous companion that can surprise us at any time. Although significant life events such as work changes, relationships, or financial difficulties are frequently recognized as stressors, there are numerous everyday elements that go unnoticed that can contribute to the accumulation of stress.

Imagine yourself as a brave adventurer, standing at the entrance to the maze that is life. There is stress wherever you look, waiting to bite you when you least expect it. Don't worry, though, as this guide will act as your reliable road map as it walks you through the complexities of stress management.

Uncovering stress's mysterious origins is necessary before one can comprehend it. Stress, that elusive frienemy, frequently shows up in your life without warning. It might have to do with impending deadlines, the unknowns of social relationships, or the ongoing pressure to live up to expectations. In this amazing fabric of life, stress is a thread that permeates everyday interactions.

As we delve further, let's bring to light for a minute, unseen elements that add to the stress symphony perpetually playing in the background of your existence. The never-ending barrage of notifications, the obsession with perfection, and the social media comparison game are all seemingly benign components but, when put together, may produce a cacophony that can leave your head spinning.

Daily Stressors: The Building Elements

1. Workplace Pressures: Today's workplaces can be extremely demanding, with short turnaround times and a never-ending to-do list. Mental health might suffer from the ongoing pressure to perform at one's best and meet expectations.

2. Technology Overload: We are inundated with messages and information in the digital age. Continuous connectivity can cause information overload, which makes it difficult to unplug and take breaks.

3. Absence of Sleep: It's common to undervalue the significance of getting enough sleep. We may wake up from a restless night feeling worn out and ill-prepared to face the stresses of the day.

4. Financial Concerns: Stress is often caused by financial concerns. Financial uncertainty, bills, and budgeting can all lead to ongoing anxiety that is detrimental to one's physical and emotional well-being.

5. Relationship Stress: Interpersonal interactions can lead to stress, whether they be with friends, family, or coworkers. Emotional strain is a result of miscommunications, disagreements, and unfulfilled expectations.

6. Academic Pressures: Teenagers and young adults face several challenges on their academic path. The pressure to maintain good grades and the demanding coursework and tests can make the school setting a haven for stress and anxiety.

7. Social Media Comparison: Stress is increased by social media's widespread influence. Feelings of inadequacy and self-doubt might arise from constantly comparing oneself to carefully managed internet personas.

8. Identity and Self-Discovery: The formative years of adolescence and early adulthood are critical for identity development and self-discovery. Emotional stress can be exacerbated by the need to fit in, societal expectations, and the search for one's identity.

9. Body Image Issues: Teenagers and young adults may experience significant mental strain due to societal norms surrounding beauty and body image. Stress levels can rise and body dissatisfaction can result from attempting to live up to excessive expectations.

10. Peer Pressure: The urge to live up to social norms and expectations from peers may be extremely stressful. Decision-making can be impacted by the need for

acceptance and the fear of judgment, which can also lead to mental distress.

11. Uncertain Future: There is doubt about future accomplishments, life objectives, and job paths during the transitional period between adolescence and maturity. One of the main sources of stress in life can be uncertainty about the future.

12. Parental Expectations: Parents' expectations about a child's academic success, profession, and personal choices can put a great deal of pressure on a person. Stress and feelings of inadequacy may be exacerbated by the urge to live up to parental expectations.

13. Time management difficulties: Juggling extracurricular activities, social obligations, academic obligations, and personal time can be difficult. Feelings of tension and overwhelm can result from ineffective time management.

14. Emotional Unrest: During adolescence, hormonal fluctuations may cause emotional unrest. Teens and young adults face daily challenges due to mood fluctuations, heightened sensitivity, and the pursuit of emotional stability.

15. Navigating Independence: The obligations that accompany becoming independent can be distressing for young people. Handling money, making decisions in life, and living with the results of decisions can all contribute to the general stress that comes with this stage of life.

Let's now discuss the components that combine to produce the ideal storm of stress. Little stressors build up over time, much like droplets make a storm cloud. Missed buses, left-over lunches, and unanswered emails may seem little individually, but when added together, they can create a pall over even the brightest of days.

Finding the triggers is essential in this adventure. What triggers your mental stress detectors? Is it the approaching tests, the intimidating social events, or the unpredictability of what lies ahead? Finding these triggers gives you the ability to foresee and, in the end, defuse the stress bomb before it explodes.

Let's now discuss strategy:

Avoiding stress entirely is not the goal of stress management because life's maze is full of unexpected turns. It's about arming yourself with the means to elegantly negotiate these turns. Think of stress as a strong river, and yourself as a proficient kayaker navigating the harsh waters using your stress-reduction techniques.

Being attentive is a useful tactic that can act as an anchor amid a wave of competing ideas and feelings. You can control the rogue stress waves that could destroy your mental health by remaining in the present. Stress-reduction techniques like deep breathing, meditation, and pausing to notice the beauty around you can be quite effective.

    a. Time Management:

Effective time management involves prioritizing tasks based on importance and urgency. Create a to-do list and categorize items as high, medium, or low priority. Break down larger projects into smaller, achievable steps, allowing you to make steady progress. Set realistic goals to avoid setting yourself up for unnecessary stress, and be flexible in adapting your schedule as needed.

b. Healthy Lifestyle:

Maintaining a healthy lifestyle is crucial for stress resilience. Regular exercise not only enhances physical health but also releases endorphins, improving mood. Balanced nutrition provides the energy and nutrients your body needs to function optimally. Ensure you get sufficient sleep to allow your mind and body to recover, promoting overall well-being.

c. Mindfulness and Relaxation Techniques:

Incorporating mindfulness practices can significantly reduce stress. Meditation helps focus the mind and cultivate a sense of calm. Deep breathing exercises, such as diaphragmatic breathing, can instantly alleviate tension. Yoga combines physical activity with mindfulness, promoting relaxation and flexibility. Regular practice of these techniques enhances your ability to cope with stressors.

d. Social Support:

Sharing your feelings with friends, family, or a therapist provides emotional support. Expressing yourself allows for a release of pent-up emotions and provides perspective on your challenges.

Surround yourself with a supportive network, fostering a sense of connection and understanding.

e. Boundaries:

Learning to say no when necessary and setting boundaries is crucial for preventing feelings of becoming overwhelmed. Understand your limits and communicate them assertively. By prioritizing your own well-being and workload, you create a healthier balance in your personal and professional life.

f. Hobbies and Leisure:

Engaging in activities you enjoy is a powerful stress management tool. Whether it's reading, painting, playing a sport, or simply spending time in nature, these activities provide a mental break and contribute to a more balanced life. Regularly scheduling leisure time allows you to recharge and maintain a positive mindset.

g. Problem Solving:

Addressing the root causes of stress involves proactive problem-solving. Identify the specific challenges contributing to your stress and brainstorm practical solutions. Break down complex problems into manageable steps, and take action to implement positive changes. Problem-solving empowers you to regain control over your circumstances and reduces ongoing stressors.

As we come to the end of our investigation into stress management, picture yourself as the commander of your ship, soaring through life's storms with fortitude and elegance. The maze could be complex, but you have the compass to lead you through it since you know what stresses and triggers cause and how to deal with them.

Stress is but one thread woven into the larger fabric of your experiences in life's vast fabrics. Accept it, comprehend it, and above all, learn how to handle it. May you have the fortitude to endure all of life's ups and downs and come out stronger, wiser, and prepared for the experiences that await you in the chapters to come.

Now that we've reached the tipping point for stress management proficiency, let's examine the idea of self-care—the lighthouse that guides us through the maze's darkest passageways. Self-care is a need, a lifeline that keeps you afloat in the middle of chaos, not a luxury. Think of it as your own arsenal, full of exercises that help you refuel your physical, mental, and emotional energy.

One often overlooks the value of taking a step back in the never-ending chase of dreams and ambitions. Think of a painter who is so focused on finishing a masterpiece that they forget to stop and enjoy the colors in their palette. Likewise, self-care is the paintbrush that adds color to the experiences on the canvas that is your life.

There are many different ways to take care of yourself, such as losing yourself in a good book, listening to relaxing music, or enjoying some alone time. These times are not frivolous pleasures; rather, they are vital investments in your health, a mental and spiritual reset.

Getting your body moving is another powerful tool in your self-care toolbox. Endorphins are released when you exercise, whether it's through a vigorous walk, yoga practice, or dance party in your living room. These activities can help lift your stress levels. Your body is a temple, so take care of it and it will be resilient in return.

Building meaningful connections is a compass that helps us navigate the maze of life. Be in the company of people who understand, encourage, and uplift you. The stagnant air of stress can be dispelled by human connection, like a soft breeze, leaving you feeling renewed and energized.

Furthermore, don't be afraid to ask for expert advice when you need it. Counselors, therapists, or mentors can be invaluable on your mental health journey, much as a ship needs experienced navigators to safely navigate dangerous waters. They can offer priceless perceptions, instruments, and insights to better prepare you for the difficulties that lie ahead.

Stress is just one note in the big symphony of life, and as the conductor, you can mold the music. Recognize that every note adds to the composition's beauty and embrace the highs and lows, crescendos, and decrescendos.